# RACING TRAINS

## THE 1895 RAILWAY RACES TO THE NORTH

*The F.W. Webb designed 0–6–2T No. 1054 passing the British Mohair Spinners Ingrow Mill, in Keighley, West Yorkshire. A large part of the mill is still in productive use, and as can be seen No. 1054 is still in fine working order 107 years after its construction.*

# RACING TRAINS

## THE 1895 RAILWAY RACES TO THE NORTH

C . D A V I D  W I L S O N

ALAN SUTTON PUBLISHING LIMITED

First published in the United Kingdom in 1995
Alan Sutton Publishing Limited
Phoenix Mill · Far Thrupp · Stroud · Gloucestershire

British Library Cataloguing-in-Publication Data

Wilson, David
  Racing Trains: 1895 Railway Races to the
  North
  I. Title
  385.0941

ISBN 0–7509–0886–6

Typeset in 11/12pt Ehrhardt.
Typesetting and origination by
Alan Sutton Publishing Limited.
Printed in Great Britain by
Hartnolls, Bodmin, Cornwall.

The driver sits there like a god,
he's a decent mate, but an idle sod.
Though I'm shovelling on my knees,
he still sits there at his ease.

Don Bilston, 'The Fireman's Song'

# CONTENTS

# ACKNOWLEDGEMENTS

I would like to thank the staff of the National Railway Museum's reading-room, David Daniels and Peter Harris of Elliff Photorail for a prompt and speedy service, Ian Allan Publishers for their kind permission to quote from a variety of sources, Eric and Mike for burning the midnight oil on the drawings, and Mohe Reiss for retrieving lost files. However, the biggest thank yous are due to Marjorie Miles and Anne Reuss for their proofreading, support, encouragement and countless cups of coffee and not a few buns.

# INTRODUCTION

Racing appears to be a universal human activity and almost anything from pigeons to clipper ships have been raced; trains are no exception. The safety conscious will doubtless be horrified that anything so rash and foolhardy could possibly have been considered, let alone undertaken. They would be aghast to know that train racing took place on the instructions of peers of the realm and under the authority of the managers of the country's largest and most powerful companies, but these men did countenance such behaviour. This book will shed some light on this activity, which, perhaps more than any other form of racing, requires the highest degree of cooperation, organization and control on the part of the participants.

The year 1995 sees the centenary of the definitive railway race, a race which created a record that still stands. In many ways it is also the centenary of the end of railway supremacy, the last heroic effort before the rot set in. New products and ideas spawned throughout the industrial revolution from 1895 onwards made deeper and deeper inroads into the two most important aspects of the railway network: distribution and communication. Paradoxically, an analogous situation is currently enveloping those systems which took over the distributive and communicative functions from the railway – road haulage and the basic telephone system, though in different ways and for very different reasons.

The growth and expansion of the railway network from 1830 onwards was arguably paralleled by a corresponding increase in control. Control of the operation of the line through the growth in signalling technology, control over increasingly large workforces via a system of sanctions and rewards, and increases in social control made possible through the more rapid deployment of troops coupled with the formation of new institutions and new legislation. New powers and technologies were giving increasing control over the forces of nature; steam had replaced sail, water and the workhorse, making human social order less dependent on the whim of nature, but increasing its dependence on the new forces, products and institutions brought about by the 'march of progress', the birth of industrial economy.

The catalyst for the growth of industrial society was the railway. The new possibilities, however mishmash and higgledy-piggledy, created by the growth of the railway network played an important role in creating the phenomenon we refer to as an industrial economy. The racing of 1895 can be seen as the high-water mark of the steam-driven Victorian industrial economy. One of the chief protagonists in the racing was at the time the largest company, with the largest factory and greatest capital of any industrial concern then in existence. This company was the London & North Western Railway. In these circumstances it is possible to regard the races as a statement about the capabilities of the company; a statement which is effectively: 'no-one is better equipped, or better organized, there are no others anywhere in the world who can compete with us'.

Making that statement and having chosen such a course, the whole effort of the organization was turned to winning. Every aspect of the company's activity was in-house: they made and laid their own rails, made their own signalling apparatus, manufactured their own steel, and they built towns, hospitals and even artificial limbs. There was nothing new to railways in the idea of racing the trains. Competitions involving speed and endurance had been part of the agenda since before this huge corporation had been founded and the product called rail travel had been established. The essential difference between the Rainhill Trials and the Races to the North is not that one involved trials and the other races, but that one was precursor and the other was last hurrah! The trials were about the use of steam power, the races of 1895 were to assert corporate authority and to hold up the corporate product and say 'ours is the best, the fastest, the most efficient railway company anywhere in the world'. The use of steam power was no longer in question.

Numerous articles have been written about the Races to the North, along with two books: a contemporaneous one by Revd W.J. Scott, and one by O.S. Nock published in the 1950s. Unlike those previous works, the context of this book lies in the recognition that what was very much a public spectacle in 1895 was by 1995 an obscure backwater in the history of Victorian railway operations. However, before consigning the races to the far shores of 'trainspotterdom', there is another line of thought along which they can be usefully followed. The public spectacle and harum-scarum train ride are one aspect, technological control and operational performance are another. The races can also be seen as a public manifestation, a true-life advertisement of the prowess and technological achievement of the steam-driven society.

New genies were about to escape the bottle as the nineteenth century ended, forces which would put an end to the steam-driven mechanics and heavy metal industries. The triple alliance of steel, coal, and railways, which in 1895 were at the height of their powers, is now a pale shadow; fewer mines, steel mills and route miles tell their own stories. The great railway workshops at Crewe shrunk to a heritage centre, ex-miners offer day-trippers a chance to see how they once shovelled and dug at seams miles underground, and once-mighty Sheffield steel is now the site of a shoppers' paradise – a huge hypermarket shopping mall. No one, not even Old Moore himself, would have imagined in 1895 that such mighty industries as coal, steel and railways would in less than a century be looked upon as industrial dinosaurs, strange artefacts of the past.

Britain in 1895 was enjoying the fruits of Empire and the benefits of having taken an early lead in the Industrial Revolution that swept Europe and North America from the last decades of the eighteenth century. The revolution had its roots in the philosophical concerns of Descartes and Newton and its first green shoots in the practical tinkerings of Newcomen and Arkwright, Compton, Watt and others. A new breed of tinkerers were coming to the fore when the races were being run: Bell, Marconi, Benz, Ford. These new names influenced the new technologies and, just as the railways before them, their new inventions changed the social world into which they were introduced.

The railway races – even the very idea now seems to belong to a different world, though modern parallels do exist – coming as they did at a time of great change and social unrest, afford the modern reader an insight into what was socially, culturally and technologically important to the populace as the Victorian age drew towards its end. The supremacy of the railway as a carrier of goods, people, communications and ideas had risen from a shaky infancy to a worldwide colossus – no developed country was without its railway system. The great benefits that the birth of the railway network afforded to the spread of ideas is only now being challenged by the spread of the global communications net and the growth of the 'information super highway'. The spread of this network is the only development in the twentieth century to come close to equalling the railway's achievements in furthering the spread of communications and ideas and forging new connections in the web of the social fabric.

The railways which so changed the public's perception had by 1895, after more than sixty years' growth, diversification and change, become old hat and a new revolution was underway. New modes of transport, new technologies of communication would spawn new corporations, bigger and more far reaching than even the railway companies had been. The changes which the railways underwent after 1895 failed to halt the inexorable growth of the new competitors, or halt the slide in their own fortunes. *Racing Trains* is about the spirit of an age when competition and survival of the fittest was the social, moral and intellectual ethos.

The ability to race trains is predicated upon having a line to race on, locomotives and rolling-stock to race with, and a team of managers, supervisors and workmen to put the order to race into practical existence. To achieve this situation requires a high degree of organization, substantial levels of investment, both of capital and labour, plus the desire and necessary authority to be able to carry such a proposition into being. That the conditions did arise and the races took place is a matter of fact; how those conditions arose and why the races took place is the subject of this book.

*Chapter One*

# THE 88

The Rainhill Trials excepted, the most famous of all the railway races were those held in the summer of 1895, involving five of Britain's then leading railway companies: the London & North Western, Caledonian, North British, North Eastern, and Great Northern Railways, thereafter referred to as the 'Railway Races to the North'. There are numerous reasons why those races can be regarded as the zenith of railway operational achievement in Great Britain.

The Liverpool and Manchester Railway staged the trials at Rainhill to determine whose locomotives would be used by the company in the actual race. Based upon speed, endurance and reliability, the competitors had to build their locomotives to comply with size and weight restrictions. Similar forms of trial also took place on the first American railways; these trials, as well as those at Rainhill, involved horse-powered, even man-powered entries, in addition to steam-powered competitors. On the day steam locomotion won out over horse power. More important, perhaps, was the creation of a precedent establishing a competitive nature into the conduct of railway life. Another feature of the trials which cannot have escaped the notice of the proprietors of the Liverpool and Manchester was the audience they drew:

> Upwards of 10,000 persons were computed to have been present, among whom were a greater number of scientific men, and practical engineers, than have ever been assembled on any previous occasion.
>
> *Liverpool Times*, 13 October 1829

The opening of lines and stations drew crowds of people to watch what was the spectacle of the age.

> The velocity with which the Novelty [the name of Braithwaite and Erickson's entry in the Rainhill Trials] moved surprised and amazed every beholder. It seemed to fly, presenting one of the most sublime spectacles of mechanical ingenuity and human daring the world ever beheld.
>
> *Liverpool Times*, 13 October 1829

By 1895 the railway was no longer the 'most sublime spectacle' and had grown to such a size that its successful operation was a far greater accomplishment than the speed of one of the locomotives, though this did have its place. There have been episodes in the long history of railways when operational achievement has verged on the heroic, for example during both the First and Second World Wars. Keeping the network open and the traffic moving during these periods was a triumph over adversity, but such episodes are not strictly comparable to the events of July and August 1895. The events of 1895, which were entirely railway created and organized operations, created huge amounts of public interest, so much so that they might even be described as railway spectaculars. Similarly, one cannot compare several weeks of racing over the length of the country with one-off flat-out dashes over fairly limited distances, such as the much-debated 100 m.p.h. sprint down Wellington Bank, performed soon after the races were held by the Great Western Railway locomotive No. 3440 *City of Truro*.

In considering the claim of the races to be the high point of railway operating in Britain, the factor which underlines the achievements of 1895 is that the network of lines and the facilities to maintain and service them constitute a 'machine', each train being but one of the machine's many thousands of moving parts. The railway does not cease to function because of the breakdown of one single train, but the failure of the permanent way or the signalling system can be the cause of very difficult problems, giving far more cause for delay to a far wider circle of services than any failure of the actual motive power – the locomotive. It is precisely because the railway network itself is a mechanical system that the achievements of 1895 are much more noteworthy than the mere rapidity of a particular locomotive on a specific journey, as for instance in the case of the Gresley Pacific No. 60022 *Mallard* and the record breaking 126 m.p.h. approaching Essendine at the bottom of Stoke Bank on the East Coast main line in July 1938.

Racing a train over a distance of more than 500 miles not once, but over a period of weeks, requires not only the ultimate in effort and performance from the footplate crews, it also requires that the whole route (in this instance the East and West Coast routes from London to Aberdeen) functions at the same peak of performance. Every yard of track, every point, every signal and every operative from the platelayer and porter upwards must also be giving of their best. The efforts of the organizational and operations staff are not subservient to the efforts on the footplate, they are the essentials which allow the train crew to fulfil their part in what is a huge team effort.

For many people living in today's cynical and safety-conscious climate, the idea of racing trains has either an almost romantic air, a kind of 'Around the World in Eighty Days' quality, or it constitutes the height of insanity and those concerned should have been removed from office. However, one hundred years on from those record-breaking August nights, it is possible to see the production of that drama in a different light.

Several commentators have remarked that the railway industry in the nineteenth century did for Britain what the automobile industry did for America in the twentieth century. To have an understanding of why some of the largest commercial undertakings, not just in Britain, but in the world, would suspend normal operations in order to hold a race, and to fully appreciate the circumstances in which those races took place, it is essential to have both a picture of how railways operate and some knowledge of railway history. Railways did not grow in isolation from daily life and because they exerted such enormous influence upon it, it is, perhaps, useful to remember that Victorian society was subject to a vastly different view of the world from that which currently prevails.

The long-running debate over which was the first 'railway' does not concern us; here it is sufficient to say that competition was an integral part of railway life. Throughout the history of railway development competitiveness was present, taking every conceivable form from the provision of buffet cars and Pullman coaches to crippling fare wars and the hijacking of locomotives. The very essence of Victorian Britain was competition – survival of the fittest (though unfortunately this is actually something of a misinterpretation, 'survival of the most fitted' is actually closer to Darwin's proposition). However, in relation to the railways, competition was fierce and there was a price to be paid for the intensity of the struggle. A look at the birth and growth of one of the competitors, the Great Northern Railway, later in this chapter illustrates this point.

Ideas about competitiveness were not solely confined to the railways. Competition was not only a concomitant part of business life, in Victorian Britain it was a major intellectual challenge; it is practically inconceivable that those men who ran the railway industry were unaffected by the issues. Darwin's book *The Origin of Species* was, for many, a treatise on the value and virtue of competition, and its publication in 1859 caused such a social, religious and political furore that many of the issues it raised were still raging thirty years on when the races were being run.

The growth of the railway as an industry gave rise to significant numbers of MPs and lords with railway interests; there were 157 members of the House of Commons and 49 members of the House of Lords with railway directorships by 1865. Equally there were no shortages of men who made their mark in the railway industry going on to become parliamentarians themselves. Robert Stephenson was for many years MP for Whitby, while another of the great railway engineers, Joseph Locke, bought the 'rotten borough' of Honiton and thus became an MP. George Hudson, the 'Railway King', was MP for Sunderland, and Samuel Morton Peto, the railway contractor, was member for Norwich. The relationship between the railways and government was far more dynamic in Victorian Britain than it is today – unfortunate though that may be – and when trying to assess the records and methods of the various companies which were the competitors in the race, the strength of their parliamentary support needs to been borne in mind.

Parliament was only one side of the coin – the other was the social fabric into which the railway companies entered. The birth of the railway network took place alongside a great deal of social unrest: anti-Corn Law agitation, Poor Law reforms, and the growth of Chartism and trade unionism were all on the social agenda. Marx's *Communist Manifesto* was first published in 1848, barely two years after the end of the first bout of Railway Mania and amid further outbreaks of Chartist rioting. There was yet another aspect of the social fabric affected by the railway progress; writing in 1844 Friedrich Engels had these comments to make:

In Manchester, the pauper burial ground lies opposite to the Old Town, along the Irk; this, too, is a rough, desolate place. About two years ago [1842] a railroad was carried through it. If it had been a respectable cemetery, how the bourgeoisie and the clergy would have shrieked over the desecration! But it was a pauper burial-ground, the resting place of the outcast and the superfluous, so no one concerned himself about the matter. It was not even thought worth while to convey the partially decayed bodies to the other side of the cemetery; they were heaped up just as it happened, and piles were driven into newly made graves, so that the water oozed out of the swampy ground, pregnant with putrifying matter, and filled the neighbourhood with the most revolting and injurious gases. The disgusting brutality which accompanied this work I cannot describe in further detail.

Engels, F., *The Condition of the Dead in 1844*,
from Legg, *The Railway Book*, p. 31

Engels's comments illustrate, in graphic terms, that railway development did not take place in a vacuum; all manner of social, economic, philosophical and political pressures shaped their development not only as technological systems, but also as hierarchical organizations of both company structures and forms of day-to-day organizational and operational control. The relationship between the development of the railway industry and alterations in the social fabric in which the industry was growing, are all too frequently reduced to anecdotes, yet, in providing a new mode of transport, the railways created a new relationship between the individual and the landscape, an entirely novel way of seeing the world and new sensations to be enjoyed in travelling over it. One need only compare the following descriptions to appreciate the huge differences between pre-railway and post-railway forms of travel:

Seated in the old mail coach we needed no evidence out of ourselves to indicate the velocity. . . . The vital experience of the glad animal sensibilities made doubts impossible on the question of our speed; we heard our speed, we saw it, we felt it as thrilling; and this speed was not the product of blind insensate agencies, that had no sympathy to give, but was incarnated in the fiery eyeballs of the noblest among brutes, in his dilated nostril, spasmodic muscles, and thunder-beating hoofs.

*Thomas de Quincey, The Collected Writings*, ed. David Masson, vol. 13, (1897),
pp. 283–4 (first published in 1849 in *Blackwood's Magazine*), from
Schivelbusch, *The Railway Journey*, pp. 11–12

. . . when proceeding on a journey by the rail-road, we are seldom allowed to get a sight of the wonderous power which draws us so rapidly along. The scene is altogether changed, there are no animals yoked to the car, to excite our pity by their apparently short, but really severe labour; we hear the steam gushing from the safety valve, while the machine is for a short time stationary; then we hear a number of rapid beatings: we feel that we are moving, the motion soon increases rapidly, and the journey which by stage-coach is so tedious, is here, long before we are aware of it, at an end. The traveller then wonders not only at the rapidity of his journey, but often wishes to inspect and comprehend the means by which it was effected.

*The Roads and Rail-Roads, Vehicles, and Modes of Travelling, of Ancient and Modern Countries . . ., 1839, p. 279, from Schivelbusch, The Railway Journey, p. 12*

The sensations of travel altered and so too did existing notions of space; the rapidity provided by rail travel shrank distances and brought places closer together in time if not in actual space. This apparent shrinkage of distances, in terms of time, created the possibility for suburban commuting and for the shipment of perishable goods over greater distances, both of which produced changes in the pattern of social life, in everything from diet to the landscape and architecture.

Growing complexity in the railway industry, the burgeoning network, and increased passenger and freight traffic all combined to stimulate the need for control technologies to manage the system: points, crossings, flyover junctions, semaphore signals and the telegraph. These emergent physical control systems were paralleled by growing efforts to increase the degree of social control, the spread of social legislation into new areas, and the creation of new social institutions or greater degrees of accountability being demanded of existing institutions. The use of military men by numerous railways to order and organize the labour force and the imposition of a growing body of working rules, staff uniforms and standardized operating procedures were all being brought into play in the attempted creation of a disciplined or self-controlled workforce, arguably an essential prerequisite for the operation of an ordered network of train control and timetabled operations.

George Findlay, who in the late 1860s became general manager of the London & North Western, insisted that:

There should be, at all times, active and vigilant supervision in every branch of the service. It is not enough that every man should be fit for his duties and trained for their performance, but it must be the duty of someone to see that he actually does perform them, and that no slackness or carelessness is allowed to supervene in carrying on the working from day to day. The railway service is pre-eminently one requiring for its efficient conduct a high degree of smartness, alacrity, energy, and zeal on the part of every individual engaged in it.

Nock, *North Western*, p. 89

To ensure that his wishes were carried into practice Findlay instituted a system of annual inspections, which covered all the departments under his control and was carried out over the whole of the London & North Western's system. The information resulting from these inspections was then used as a criteria for promotion or as suggestions for improvements in working practices. The creation of organized systems of information gathering was an important step in being able to effect control over rapidly expanding organizations, with growing numbers of employees and larger and more complex ranges of operational problems to be overcome.

The benefits afforded by the railway, for the physical control of civil society, were not lost on the government who used the newly opened London & Birmingham and Grand Junction Railways to move troops from the south to quell riots in the Potteries and East Lancashire. In these circumstances the railway can be seen as an essential part of the government's ability at that time to govern, and the men who owned and controlled the railways were, as has been shown, an important element within the Victorian ruling class, in so far as they represented significant power blocks within parliament and the Lords. In addition to their position as major political power blocks, the railway barons were leading industrial players in control of large workforces; there were for instance, during periods of railway booms, more men employed as navvies than were enlisted in the army and navy combined.

The railway, in addition to its role in the increase in the ordering and regimentation of social life, also played a part in bringing technology to warfare in 1859, when British navvies, supplies and equipment were shipped out from Liverpool to build a line to take ammunition and supplies to the front at Sebastopol, arguably saving the British Army from further embarrassment at the hands of an enemy who had the temerity to shoot the Light Brigade to ribbons. The historian A.J.P. Taylor put forward convincing arguments for the influence of the German railway timetable on the decision to mobilize and commence hostilities in the First World War, further proof, if any was needed, of the importance of the link between the State and the railway.

Between 1830 and 1850 5,000 miles or more of railway were constructed and by the mid-1860s almost two-thirds of what was to become the total British railway network was constructed – the growth of the competing companies had been consolidated. However, the rise of the railway industry should not be viewed as being solely one of the physical achievement involved in laying tracks across the country and building the locomotives and rolling-stock to utilize on them. The very novelty of the railway should be remembered; as an industry it was one which was largely devoid of any form of precedent. The lack of precedents took numerous guises: initially the Stockton & Darlington allowed common use of its tracks. This practice led to disputes over track occupation with trains travelling in opposite directions on the same line, and so on. The result was near chaos as even these most basic levels of operation had to be worked out by trial and error.

The changes in practice which led to the railway operating company becoming the provider of the locomotive power, if not the rolling-stock, came to the fore both as the number of routes and route mileages grew, and in order to minimize the sort of problems which had been encountered on the Stockton & Darlington. Another significant element in the changes were problems that arose through the need for maintenance or running repairs. In an age when standardization had hardly been considered, regular maintenance was not quite the routine task it became after improvements such as those which occurred with the introduction of the Whitworth standard thread, or as a result of the activities of the

Manchester Society for the Prevention of Boiler Explosions, whose systematic approach to boiler safety and maintenance is still in current practice – boiler inspection is still essential when obtaining boiler insurance. It was these types of day-to-day practicalities that came to influence the methods of operation chosen by each company in respect of its own operational peculiarities, and in the same way they created institutions to administer and regulate the new technology, putting ever greater degrees of control in the hands of human agency.

Operating the railways in their infancy was further complicated by the material quality and mechanical reliability of the available technology and by some of the operating conditions that were allowed to flourish. The gentry and nobility frequently had their own coaches lashed to trucks and coupled to the train, along with their own horseboxes. These practices not only caused inordinate amounts of delay, they also carried other hazards most commonly associated with lack of or only rudimentary forms of maintenance – broken couplings and a general lack of braking arrangements being the most common sources of accidents on the fledgling network. Inevitably these practices led to there being serious injury and loss of life. When this situation could no longer be tolerated, legislation was forthcoming to remedy the shortcomings. This organic style of the growth of operational control was very much the manner by which rail travel ultimately became the safest mode of land transport.

It was not only the railway which was undergoing rapid change and development between 1830 and 1850 – the same period also saw large rises in the production and output of other industries. However, it is very noticeable that two industries in particular show very marked growth: iron output doubled between 1835 and 1850, and coal production rose from 23 million tons in 1830 to 65 million tons in 1856. This period also saw a near doubling of export trade, growth in textile manufacture and increased mechanization in almost every aspect of manufacture. The railway's place in all this was not just as a consumer of iron and coal, but also as a facilitator, bringing down transport costs, opening up new markets and encouraging mobility and the spread of ideas. This latter quality is one which is seldom regarded and yet had enormous potential, for the spread of ideas stimulates all other conditions.

Throughout the early years of railway growth, the need for effective competition was seen as vital, and parliament and most vested interests were strongly anti-monopoly. These two tendencies must shoulder much of the responsibility for the eventual shape of the British railway network prior to the 'rationalization' of Beeching and after. Similarly, the financial difficulties created by the duplication of routes and almost ruinous competition for traffic, which in some instances barely justified one route let alone two and sometimes more, is the consequence of this particular form of unbridled and unregulated industrial growth. A more planned and organized growth would not only have avoided ruinous competition but would also have had the benefit of lowering construction costs for the routes that were built.

Railway promotion in Britain was carried on entirely by private enterprise. Although six major Government Committees discussed railway policy between 1839 and 1853, laissez-faire had bitten deeply, and only one of these Committees – Gladstone's of 1844 – recommended even a gradual taking over of railways by the State. So this important service was left to grow up haphazard, at the whim of private profit. While in France and Germany the railway system was planned, in Britain there existed no system, but simply many miles of railway lines, for the most part following existing lines of communication.

Gregg, Social and Economic History, p. 102

Gladstone, as president of the Board of Trade, took an interest in railway affairs and also provided the government with powers to buy up all the railways they sanctioned, after a twenty-one year period, though they were never exercised. Other powers enacted in early railway legislation enabled the government to demand that the railways reduce their charges if they paid a dividend of more than 10 per cent for three consecutive years. There were powers which made it a requirement to carry third-class passengers, though this was something of a quid pro quo; the railways had to carry the third-class passenger, though not by all services, and they did not have to charge passenger duty on them. It was these services, upon which the third-class passengers were conveyed, that came to be known as 'Parliamentaries'. Passenger duty or Travellers' Tax, a tax on passengers, was enacted as early as 1832 and more than sixty years elapsed before Travellers' Tax was finally laid to rest.

Railway development in Britain was an almost ceaseless debate about which was the better way first to inaugurate and then develop the network. The clauses in the 1844 Railway Regulation Bill, which gave the government powers to curtail dividends, enforce the carriage of certain categories of passenger and purchase the railways they sanctioned, can be seen as an early indicator of the scepticism surrounding the notion of untrammelled rivalry, creating the most desirable of outcomes. Another pointer to the levels of opposition to *laissez-faire* growth is the large number of entries on this topic in Ottley's *Bibliography of British Railway History*. There are almost five hundred references in the section dealing with railways and the nation, which rises to more than five hundred when historical works are taken into consideration. The bulk of these references concern issues of the control of railways, with many being directly related to the formation of a coherent strategy for the growth, management and ownership of the national network.

The method of railway promotion and construction in Britain added considerably to the costs per mile of line built, as the following quotes from the foremost exponents of railway engineering and contracting attest. When considering these quotes it is perhaps worth remembering that both the individuals concerned (Locke and Brassey) were also responsible for the construction and engineering of lines on several continents, and thus had almost unique knowledge of the various methods of railway promotion, financing, engineering and construction. Until 1848 Brassey was the largest contractor at work on French railway projects, with over 5,000 British navvies shipped over to France to work on his contracts.

Although France possessed most of the prerequisites for a major programme of railway building – National Unity, political stability, expanding manufactures, etc. – there was a shortage of capital for investment and largely for that reason the Government in France (and in most other continental states) played a larger part in railway construction from the beginning. In Britain free enterprise was almost total. Railways required an Act of Parliament – incidentally a time wasting and expensive procedure which, according to Joseph Locke, could absorb 25 per cent of the railway company's subscribed capital – but the government exercised no control over where or when railways should be built. . . .

Brassey used to say that French Railways were better run, their carriages more comfortable, their stations more adequate and their supervision generally more competent.

Mountfield, The Railway Barons, pp. 83–4, 85

The bill for the Great Northern's Royal Assent has been put at £433,000, a sum which would, at the time, have built 60 miles of railway on the Continent and one cannot help wondering at the differences in cost and the effects upon them of the differing methods employed in creating the railway infrastructure. The former of the two quotes above suggests that the reason for the difference between the British and Continental methods of railway finance was the availability of capital in Britain and the lack of it in the European states. However, the availability of capital is scarcely a reason for adopting laissez-faire attitudes to where, when, and how railway building would proceed. It is also possible to say that the availability of capital, or lack of it, was behind the boom and bust nature of British railway construction and that this too imposed a financial toll.

Yet the story of the railways is in some respects a seamy saga. On the one hand, a magnificent engineering epic, on the other, a tangled swamp of dubious planning, rougeish [*sic*] financing, opportunism, speculation and fraud.

Mountfield, The Railway Barons, p. 8

The whole question of railway promotion is littered with failed schemes and over-engineered and overambitious routes, and from the evidence available one may well arrive at the conclusion that huge amounts of time, money, materials and effort were wasted. This is not to mention lives lost, or livelihoods ruined through injury. Despite the elapse of more than sixty years between the opening of the Liverpool and Manchester Railway in 1830 and the races of 1895, railway ownership, control and promotion were still an important topic. In addition to a constant debate about ownership there was also a persistent argument about the wasteful consequences of unfettered competition. The interesting point here, which will be dealt with in more detail in chapter six, is that in spite of the enormous changes that have occurred to the nation's transport infrastructure, especially the decline in rail traffic over the last fifty years, the issue of ownership and control is still the current form of railway debate in 1995.

In the classic British tradition, twenty-five years after the first of the great railway amalgamations, which were in the process of creating regional monopolies, a parliamentary committee was deliberating on the effects of amalgamations. Their findings were that, on the whole, amalgamations were a good thing and in the case of one of the railways involved in the races, the North Eastern Railway, they had led to lower rates and fares and higher levels of dividends – the classic 'win, win' situation.

The Board of Trade had, up to 1845, maintained a position which was to the effect that so long as existing lines kept their fares at reasonable levels, they, the Board of Trade, would not sanction new directly competing routes, a deal which had been accepted by most of the leading companies. Then in June 1845 Peel, who was Prime Minister, overturned one of the board's decisions and the system of self-control and regulation dissolved. The only tangible benefit flowing from Peel's overturning of the board's decision was the resolution of the gauge debate in favour of 4 ft 8½ in, though it was a further forty-five years before the broad gauge was dismantled.

The years from 1844 to 1846, commonly known as Railway Mania, were a period in railway history when speculators could boast of making fortunes between breakfast and suppertime, by dealing in railway company shares. The naming of someone like Locke as engineer, or the objections of someone like Hudson could add or subtract pounds from the value of a company's shares. George Hudson was extremely influential in matters of railway-share dealings during this period and his wheelings and dealings both in and out of parliament were followed intently, by railway promoters and speculators alike. Share trading was a new phenomenon in Victorian Britain, as M.C. Reed comments:

> The buying and selling of shares, unimportant before the coming of the railway, was an essential part of the Victorian commercial structure.
>
> Reed, *Railways in the Victorian Economy*, p. 183

These changes in financial behaviour were not confined to the rich and titled. The growth in trade and manufacture which had been progressing steadily from the 1770s had spawned a growing and relatively affluent middle class and it was the railways which created the circumstances in which this group could invest some of the savings they were beginning to accumulate.

> To finance industry on the scale necessary to the Industrial Revolution it remained necessary to mobilize the savings which still lay in banks or which were hoarded at home. The high interest paid, particularly by the railways, was partially successful in making available this capital. . . .
>
> It was no longer necessary to invest thousands of pounds; anyone with savings, however small, was welcomed by the railway promoters. The small investor had come into the field, and with him the small savings of the country were for the first time mobilized.
>
> Gregg, *Social and Economic History*, pp. 118, 101

The methods and traditions of railway practice in the late nineteenth century were all being forged in the performances, antagonisms and organizational imperatives of the 1840s and '50s. The solutions which were worked out during these formative years had to cover all aspects of the railway industry from the raising of capital to the operation of the route, and each set of new methods of working grew in response to practical difficulties. The Railway Clearing House opened for business in 1842. Based on the banking clearing house system, it was the practical response to the difficulties of distributing revenues between companies who, in addition to their individualistic policies on operational matters, were equally independent in the accounting procedures they adopted. The difficulty with accounting methods and the through-booking of passenger and freight traffic, which began to grow with the formation of a network as opposed to a series of lines, made the need for an organization like the clearing house essential.

The need to find new sources of capital, initially through share issues, with which to build the railways led to a growth in share trading which Reed remarked upon. The knock-on effect of this change in fiscal habits is that the railway industry is credited with being the *raison d'être* for the opening of the regional stock exchanges in the cities of Liverpool and Manchester in 1836, a boom year for railways. The mania of the mid-1840s saw further exchanges opened in many large provincial cities, Leeds, Glasgow and Birmingham being among the first.

*The earliest forms of signals were by modern standards very crude. This early Great Western Railway signal has pulleys and wires that moved the signal so that either the slotted bar or the disc above it was facing the driver. Similarly, the lamp positioned below the slotted bar could also be rotated to give clear or danger signals after dark.*

Conversely the railway also played a part in their gradual decline – mostly due to speedier communications, both physically by rail and electronically via the growing telegraph system developed as part of the control system dealing with the movement of trains on the expanding railway network.

To these examples of new institutional forms we could add such intangibles as the standardization of time made necessary by the operational requirements of the timetabling of services, and perhaps more importantly the adoption and adaptation of the electric telegraph as a means of providing a safe method of train control which reduced the likelihood of accidental collision.

The first uses of telegraphy for train control were at Clay Cross tunnel in Derbyshire and at New Cross in south London, both in 1841. When the races were run, the telegraph and the telegram were still the only means of rapid long-distance communication, though the telephone system was poised for take-off. The adoption of the telegraph for train control was a classic example of the 'invention awaiting an application'. The theory of electromagnetic induction was put forth by Faraday in 1831, only months after the opening of the Liverpool and Manchester Railway. The adoption of the telegraph was not a complete panacea for the problems of train control, but it was a major step forward. Safe working practices took years to inaugurate. All too often, these practices only came about after some major incident and at the intervention of the railway inspectorate.

Like the clearing house and the stock exchanges, the Railway Inspectorate was another institution which grew specifically in response to the growth of the railway business. Initially a subdivision of the Board of Trade, the Railway Inspectorate survived as a single entity until 1992 when it was absorbed into the Health & Safety Executive – a move which is felt by many will undermine the quality and quantity of specialized knowledge brought to bear on railway accidents and mishaps. However, it would be fair to say that railways and governments have a long and chequered history and this is just another episode, in what at times has been a very unsavoury and often unproductive relationship.

The adoption of safe operating procedures and the use of the safest types of equipment, was an area of railway practice which was subject to a great deal of argument and error. This aspect of railway affairs was frequently less than consistent and was all too often influenced only by legal interference, either directly via parliamentary legislation or indirectly through such ancient forms as the 'deodand'. This was a variety of Middle Ages insurance cover which could be imposed by the Coroners Court and resulted in the railway company being forced to pay compensation to those they had injured or wronged in order to recover their goods, rolling-stock or locomotive, which would have been impounded by the Coroners Court.

Incredibly, even in such a seemingly important issue as passenger safety, the idiosyncrasies of the chairman or chief engineer or the parsimony of the Board of Directors played their part. It is sad to say that all too frequently the safest methods of working and the safest equipment only came into being, or use, when some major incident made the changes or incorporations inevitable and to satisfy public disquiet. Moreover, it is not too difficult to argue the case that even to this day, this form of progress is still very much the way of things.

In the very early days some railways competed by making the traveller's life as difficult as possible, with lack of connections being a deliberate policy. This practice in some instances carried on far longer than could be considered good business practice. That it happened at all is a sign that not everyone involved with the railways initially viewed them as a network. The piecemeal growth of the railway network in Britain, influenced by motives of profit, and utilizing all manner of protectionist and spoiling tactics, exposed many of the flaws of leaving infrastructure development to 'market forces'. This manner of growth was costly and time-consuming; the expense of repeated surveys and fighting parliamentary bills clause by clause, and line by line, added significantly to legal fees, all of which inflated the cost per mile of line built, as did more mundane and practical matters such as the terrain, the type of soil, and even the weather.

The construction of Britain's main line railways varied in cost from as little as £10,000 per mile to more than £40,000. Sometimes these huge differences were attributable to the terrain, in other cases to the incompetence of, or lack of, suitable precedents for the engineers, surveyors and contractors. In the case of the London & North Western's line from London out to Rugby, originally the London & Birmingham Railway's main line, the demand for a ruling gradient not exceeding 1 in 330 meant the construction of expensive earthworks, cuttings, and embankments to keep to this demand. This line, one of the very earliest, was engineered to this standard, at least in part, as disputes still existed about the efficiency of adhesion and the limitations of locomotive technology, because of the engineer's and the board's own prejudices. Other routes and even other sections of what eventually became the London & North Western's route to Carlisle were built to less exacting standards of gradient, though they naturally became more exacting on the locomotives.

Complementing the physical, social and institutional changes was a growing public interest in railway affairs, which from the very beginning grew to such an extent that a specialist press was created to meet the demands for information on all aspects of railway affairs. Herapath's *Railway Magazine* was published as early as 1835 and the *Railway Times* first appeared in 1837, whereas *The Times* of London had been giving coverage to railway issues since 1825, the year of the 'Panic' in which more than sixty banks failed. *The Economist* carried a special section covering railway issues from 1845 onwards. The growing railway network had another effect on the nature and transmission of information, namely the ability to provide transportation of sufficient speed as to make a national daily paper possible. This possibility was not lost on the owners of a newsagents business that went on to became a household name: W.H. Smith.

In 1847 Smith's chartered a special train to carry newspapers from Euston to Scotland; the journey was by rail to the limits of the newly formed Caledonian Railway at Beattock – then over a turnpike road to Glasgow. The Euston–Beattock journey was made at an average speed of 40 m.p.h. excluding stops. The following year, 1848, Smith's again chartered a special train this time running over the then East Coast route, for which an average speed of some 49 m.p.h. was claimed, for the London–Edinburgh journey. The determination to generate new business based on speed of service is present in this episode.

Though this event was a one-off special hired by a customer of the railway, it does indicate quite well the changing commercial possibilities being brought about by the expansion of route mileage and the increased speeds and reliability of service.

Returning to the factors governing the organic growth of both the lines and the operational practices upon them, it can be seen that the temperamental and unreliable nature of early locomotives required that the men who drove them needed some knowledge of their workings and that they be competent to effect minor adjustments or repairs. These requirements at first led to there being a preponderance of north-easterners among the early railwaymen. North-eastern England, in particular the coalfields of Durham, Northumberland and Yorkshire, were the scene of most of the early experimentation with steam traction and as a result there were men in these areas with the requisite skills. The social standing and esteem afforded to the early footplatemen gave them a status not unlike that of the twentieth-century airline pilot – indeed there are many references in the literature of the railway's infancy to rail travel being like 'flight' and to 'rushing through the air'. The standing of the enginemen and their loyalty to the company that employed them has often been referred to. There is, however, no shortage of evidence to suggest that relations between employed and employer were not always harmonious.

Two issues referred to previously, the unreliability of locomotive technology and the practice of adding more and more vehicles to the train, resulted in the frequent use of multiple locomotive working of single trains. These factors had their repercussions on company policy, in employment and in locomotive practice. The company most usually associated with a small engine policy and the use of multi-locomotive haulage was the Midland, but the London & North Western was also prone to this method of operation, though part of its policy of not having express services exceeding 40 m.p.h. would also qualify as a contributory factor in its small engine policy. Another competitor, the Great Northern, eschewed this policy as far as humanly possible. These responses and solutions to what are basically operational decisions came to be incorporated into practices which in turn affected subsequent operating practice.

There are several reasons why the Great Northern did not favour the small engine policy, perhaps foremost among them that, not having been given parliamentary consent until 1846, they had the benefit of hindsight and a growing body of precedent and expertise upon which to draw. It is also possible that the attitude of the Board of Directors and the instructions to the man it appointed as locomotive engineer had more than a little to do with the rejection of the small engine policy.

The man chosen by the Great Northern, Archibald Sturrock, had served his apprenticeship with Daniel Gooch up in Dundee and when Gooch went to Swindon he invited Sturrock to join him. The locomotives being built at Swindon were broad gauge locomotives. It would doubtless have seemed to Sturrock that the designs he drew up for the Great Northern were small engines, as by comparison with the broad gauge they were, though of course they were not so, relative to the standard gauge engines of the day. There was another facet of Sturrock's work which is worth mentioning here – he increased the boiler pressure of his engines to 150 p.s.i., which was on average 50 per cent higher than anything currently being used. It could be argued that from the very outset the Great Northern had every intention of winning trade by offering a fast service and that the appointment of Sturrock and the instructions to him follow from that choice.

Despite almost continuous competition and at times bitter rivalry, a certain amount of cooperation was forthcoming, if circumstances demanded. The Forth Bridge, which plays its own part in the races of 1895, was financed by the North British, North Eastern, Great Northern and Midland Railways, with the Midland paying the lion's share. One can appreciate the cooperation between the North British, North Eastern and Great Northern, after all the bridge was deep in North British territory, which, together with the North Eastern and the Great Northern, was offering a direct service from London to Aberdeen. Benefits to the Midland appear no greater than those of the other companies. If one considers the areas of potential conflict in any relationship between the Midland, Great Northern and North Eastern, then there were no shortages of potential for disputes and rivalries.

In Scotland the Midland was frequently associated with cooperating with the Glasgow & South Western Railway, though it had long had links with the North British through the involvement of George Hudson, who put £50,000 of his York & North Midland Railway's money into the capital of the North British in 1844 when the North British was still in the process of obtaining the Royal Assent. In 1844 the York & North Midland was still part of the Hudson empire, along with those companies under his control which became the basis of the amalgamation that formed the Midland Railway. In 1875 when the Settle–Carlisle route opened, the Midland Railway began a service to Edinburgh over the North British line from Carlisle, the 'Waverley' route, a service which also carried what was then the latest version of inter-railway rivalry: the Pullman car. Despite the longevity of the relationship between the North British and the Midland and the gains in through-running for the Midland's traffic to Aberdeen, it is difficult to see any sound commercial reason for the Midland to put up the greater part of the construction costs of the Forth Bridge.

Of the five competitors, the North British was perhaps the weakest and its relations with the North Eastern were not always as cooperative as joint bridge building enterprises might suggest. The North British was, for reasons known only to itself, overly eager to have its own route into Newcastle and in 1862 a chance to gain that access occurred when the North Eastern Railway sought to amalgamate the Newcastle & Carlisle. The eventual accommodation, which secured the deal for the North Eastern, was that if the North Eastern were to give access to the North British into Newcastle via the Newcastle & Carlisle's metals, then the North British would withdraw its objections and at the same time give the North Eastern running powers from its junction with the North British at Berwick-upon-Tweed into Edinburgh. Seven years later in 1869 the North Eastern, in conjunction with the Great Northern, used this access and running powers to good effect.

That same year, 1869, saw the opening of the North British Railway's route from Edinburgh to Carlisle. The North British immediately began to send its freight services via this route and then over the London & North Western to London instead of over the North Eastern route. Just how much of this form of cat and mouse style of management was due to personalities and what proportion was good business practice it is difficult to assess. However, the North Eastern was a much larger and more profitable railway than the North British and it may have seemed prudent to the board of the North British to keep the North Eastern at arms length, from the point of view of maintaining its own independence.

The North Eastern, in association with the Great Northern, chose this very juncture, 2 August 1869 (only ten days before the opening of the grouse season), to announce the commencement of a new service from King's Cross to Edinburgh, departing King's Cross at 8 p.m. and arriving in Edinburgh at 6.05 a.m. Not only was this a new service, but the North Eastern exercised its running powers over the North British and used its own locomotives throughout on the Newcastle–Edinburgh journey. This episode is yet more tangible evidence of a contest for the London–Edinburgh traffic based on speed of service. In view of previous rivalries and subsequent events it seems hardly surprising that the London & North Western/Caledonian partnership responded with its own 8 p.m. service from Euston to Edinburgh.

These little incidents also show how fickle the North British could be and how any alteration or improvement of services would be responded to. However, we are getting ahead of schedule and there are events taking place during the 1840s and '50s that need to be considered before going any further. Three of the five competitors began their histories in the 1840s; the North British and Great Northern were in the process of obtaining parliamentary sanctions in 1844, and the Caledonian commenced services as far as Beattock in 1847. The North Eastern Railway was created by the same process of amalgamation in 1854, as the London & North Western had been in 1846, which occurred at the same time as the opening of the Lancaster–Carlisle section of the race route.

This route, along with that of the Grand Junction to the south, was engineered by Joseph Locke. Locke was the most cost effective of the early railway engineers, and was for a period retained by the promoters of the London & York (the name under which the Great Northern was put before parliament). Locke was to survey the route, though he was destined not to take any further part. At that time he was chief engineer to the Grand Junction and as a direct result of the growing rivalry between the so–called 'Euston Confederacy' and the London & York scheme, Locke was obliged to give way in his post with the London & York. The association of names with particular projects had important consequences, for the linking of names could help to ensure safe passage for a bill through parliament or ensure the success of a share issue and could, therefore, be essential to any scheme's successful completion.

The sheer volume of parliamentary proceedings attributable to railway matters can be gauged from the fact that between 1835 and 1899 railway petitions to parliament generated some 3,500 volumes of up to 2,000 pages each. Parliament set up a Select Committee to deal with railway questions in 1839, which in 1840 produced the Railway Regulations Act and inaugurated the previously mentioned Railway Inspectorate, though at this point in time it was still only a subdivision of the Board of Trade. An officer of the Royal Engineers was co-opted onto the committee and others were used as inspectors. This established something of a tradition within the Railway Inspectorate in which most of the important posts were held by members of the officer class, and often from those who had had service with the Royal Engineers or later the Transport Corps.

It was in the middle of the greatest of the railway booms, and amid the creation of conditions for new forms of trade and commerce that the Great Northern Railway began its life. The proposals for the London & York represented the most ambitious railway plans then put before a parliament, and in one of those little coincidences, which often seem to owe more to conspiracy than chance, the man credited with swaying the arguments in favour of the granting of the London & York Bill was another famous railway name, Joseph Pease, son of Edward Pease, the benefactor of the Stockton & Darlington.

In 1844 when the London & York proposals for 327 miles of tracks, with a capital of £4.5 million, were launched they undoubtedly represented the most serious threat to the companies then operating services to the north of England. These were the London & Birmingham, Grand Junction and Liverpool & Manchester Railways, which, two years later in 1846, amalgamated to form the London & North Western and those companies owned or controlled by George Hudson, which covered the route via Rugby, Leicester, Derby, Sheffield and Normanton to York. Subsequently these lines became part of the Midland Railway.

These companies did everything in their not-inconsiderable power to thwart the efforts of the London & York proposals and when parliamentary moves and delays failed to halt the passage of the London & York Bill, other tactics were used. From the launch of its prospectus in 1844 the London & York took until 1846 to gain the Royal Assent. Hudson's delaying tactics held up the legal formation of the Great Northern, but once the bill had gained its passage and work commenced on the construction Hudson and his co-conspirators at Euston began to put more concrete obstacles in the way of the Great Northern's progress.

Hudson was able to exploit existing powers to open a line into Peterborough, getting there before the Great Northern. Captain Mark Huish, general manager of the London & North Western, aided and abetted by Hudson and others, was able to ensure traffic pooling arrangements which severely disadvantaged the Great Northern, the so-called 'Octuple Agreement'. That this arrangement was limited to five years' duration was much to the credit of Edmund Denison, chairman and chief architect of the proposals which led to the creation of the Great Northern. However, despite the best efforts of Huish and Hudson the Great Northern did begin to prosper and, as Pease had predicted in his evidence to the Select Committee, the opening of the route had led to a drop in coal prices in London from £1.50 per ton to just 85p. Setting the cat firmly among the pigeons, Queen Victoria herself used the Great Northern to journey to Balmoral in 1851.

The following year the Great Northern opened its new terminus at King's Cross, half a mile from the enemy camp at Euston, and it finally completed and opened the direct route between Peterborough and Retford. Previously the route to Doncaster had been via Peterborough, Boston and Lincoln to Retford, a journey no shorter than the one that they had intended to replace (that of Hudson's via Rugby, Leicester, Derby, etc.). However, from 1852 onwards with the through-route open the Great Northern had the advantage and four years later this advantage was to prove most important.

Early in 1856 a fares war over the routes to London from the Midlands and the Eastern Counties began, but instead of creating difficulties for the Great Northern, the war resulted in a rise in traffic for all concerned and in particular for the Great Northern, who gained most of the new business because they had the faster services. Fare cutting and its equivalent, alterations to the classes of travel, were a feature of railway operations which along with the promotion of special services and excursions led to increasing numbers of people using the railways. It has to be said, however, that these are not altruistic events, and the pursuit of profit and the provision of dividends to shareholders were the main concern of the railway directors.

In the twelve-year period between the original prospectus of the London & York and the fares war of 1856 almost every possible form of difficulty had been created in an attempt to undermine the Great Northern. It could scarcely have come as a surprise to Huish, when he proposed that the London & North Western and the Great Northern come to a deal over territory in 1857, that not only did he receive a rebuff, but that he also had to sit back and watch as the Great Northern entered into agreements with the Manchester, Sheffield & Lincoln Railway. This arrangement allowed the Great Northern access into Manchester, the very heart of London & North Western territory.

There is a hint of the races of 1895 in this episode. Both routes shared the theme of a common junction. The entry to London Road, Manchester, was the important point in 1857 and Kinnaber Junction was the critical junction on the Aberdeen road in 1895. Despite having the more difficult and longer route, the Great Northern made a point of being first to Manchester especially during the first few weeks of operation. However, in the 1895 races the positions were reversed, with the London & North Western having the longer route and arriving first in Aberdeen.

The antagonism between the Great Northern and the London & North Western has its mirror image north of the border. There the two Scottish competitors, the North British and the Caledonian, were involved in very similar forms of internecine strife over traffic to Carlisle, in and around the cities of Glasgow and Edinburgh, through to Fife and the route to Aberdeen, indeed the section from Kinnaber Junction to Aberdeen was Caledonian metals. Before proceeding to outline the development of the Scottish competitors there are a number of other issues concerning the English companies which need to be discussed.

Following the amalgamation of the London & Birmingham, Grand Junction and Liverpool & Manchester Railways into the London & North Western, one of its first moves was to incorporate the Lancaster & Carlisle and the Preston Junction Railways, thus establishing its route from London to Carlisle. This is often cited as the basis for the London & North Western's claim to the title 'Premier Line' – this and the fact that it incorporated the Liverpool & Manchester.

There seems little doubt that the growth of the London & North Western was quite staggering, even by modern standards. Following its creation in 1846 the next twenty years saw it rise to become the world's largest company with over 60,000 employees. The towns of Wolverton and Crewe, though the former was begun by the London & Birmingham and the latter was inaugurated by the Grand Junction, came under the virtual ownership of the London & North Western along with the huge railway workshops in them. The company had also used its near monopolistic position to good effect, particularly in holding down the speeds of its express services and thus saving on operating costs. Sadly it had also used its monopoly to resist such items as improvements to train braking systems.

Like the London & North Western, the North Eastern Railway was formed through the amalgamation of several earlier lines and, like the London & North Western, over a number of years it grew through amalgamations to incorporate some seventy-four companies both public and private, as well as being a partner in ten joint lines. Some of the eventual constituents of the North Eastern have histories pre-dating or at least paralleling that of the Liverpool & Manchester, which doubtless led them to contend the London & North Western's premiership claims.

At the time of the races the North Eastern was responsible for the York–Edinburgh section of the race route, though the Berwick-upon-Tweed–Edinburgh section belonged to the North British with the North Eastern providing motive power, exercising the rights gained in 1862 and in general usage since 1869. However, even this apparently long-standing arrangement was not without friction and in 1894 there began a dispute between the two companies, which was still bubbling during the race period itself and was not finally resolved until 1898.

The dispute concerned the North Eastern's running powers into Edinburgh where, in 1894, the North British was about to remodel Waverley station. The North British decided that only their locomotives were to be allowed into the new station and this meant that the North Eastern would not be able to run through from Newcastle. The North Eastern refused to accept the ultimatum and the North British went to the Railways and Canal Commission to force compliance. However, the Commission found in favour of the North Eastern, but the North British were so reluctant to back down that they went as far as to the House of Lords for a remedy, which only sent them back to the Commission.

Eventually a compromise deal was worked out, but not before the North British had spent a year running the services between Edinburgh and the south, as far as Berwick-upon-Tweed, with their own locomotives, thus enforcing a break of journey which prior to this had, on many services, been non-stop. The North British even had to double-head some of the heavier trains to allow for the engine changes to be accommodated within the existing timetables, which undoubtedly drove up costs. It also cost the North British revenue, as the North

Eastern began an arrangement with the Caledonian to route Glasgow-bound passengers via the Newcastle–Carlisle line and then over Caledonian metals to Glasgow, actually a shorter route by about ten miles. That the companies were actively cooperating in the races during the course of this dispute was a strange anomaly; it may also account for some of the delays to the racing train, which occurred occasionally at Waverley.

Discussing the events of 1894–8 has run way ahead of that of the history of the North Eastern Railway, to which it is necessary to return. The North Eastern Railway was, as was mentioned above, responsible for the lines stretching from York to Berwick, which were incorporated as the York, Newcastle & Berwick Railway in 1847. The York–Darlington section opened under the title of the Great North of England Railway and had its own rather unique claim to fame. The unscrupulous methods used by George Hudson to obtain control of this line led, eventually, to his downfall.

The whole idea of the York–Newcastle line was launched in 1835 and it was planned to begin with the building of the Newcastle–Darlington section. There had been a survey by George Stephenson and the line was championed by Edward Pease of the Stockton & Darlington. The events which surround this venture could well be the reason why Pease supported the application for the London & York Bill in 1844. The Great North of England received Royal Assent for its Newcastle–Darlington section in 1836 and the York–Darlington section one year later. However, work began first on the southern part of the line at Croft and the whole York–Darlington section opened in 1841. There was, however, a fly in the ointment. In building the York–Darlington line the company had expended all its capital and another company had been formed to build the Newcastle–Darlington part of the route.

The new proposals for the Newcastle–Darlington line caused a rift between Pease and Hudson, apparently because Hudson refused to incorporate part of the Stockton & Darlington line into the new route, especially as the Great North of England, which opened the York–Darlington portion of the route, was initially inspired by the Stockton & Darlington and benefited from the Stockton & Darlington's engineering expertise. Though Hudson got his way with the proposed railway line and even succeeded in gaining control of the Great North of England Railway, it was his undoing and by 1850 Hudson's influence on railway affairs was at an end. Before entirely dismissing Hudson as a charlatan and fraudster it is perhaps worth remarking that Gladstone had this to say of him:

> It is a great mistake to look back upon him [Hudson] as a speculator. He was a man of great discernment, possessing a great deal of courage and rich enterprise – a very bold and not unwise projector.
>
> Allen, *The North Eastern Railway*, p. 97

Before his demise Hudson was also involved in the Newcastle–Berwick–Edinburgh portion of the race route. Hudson's first involvement was, as we have discovered, in having his York & North Midland Railway invest £50,000 in the proposed Edinburgh–Berwick route of the 'Great North British Railway', subsequently North British Railway. The second of Hudson's involvements was his chairmanship of, and activities in, the incorporation of the Newcastle & Berwick Railway which was given Royal Assent in 1845. The Newcastle–Berwick route was opened in 1847, as was the North British route from Edinburgh to Berwick; it was, though, a further three years before both the Tweed and Tyne were bridged and the direct rail link finally established.

The bridge over the Tweed at Berwick was opened by Her Majesty Queen Victoria and was henceforth known as the Royal Border Bridge. On the same day, 29 August 1850, Victoria had also opened the new Newcastle Central station, and one year earlier Victoria had again been on hand to open the High Level bridge over the Tyne, though neither Tyne bridge nor Newcastle station were given the 'Royal' appellation. At the time of the opening of the through-route, access to Newcastle from the south was still that formed by the Newcastle & Darlington Junction Railway, the more direct Team Valley route between Gateshead and Durham not being fully opened until 1868. The shortening of the route south of Durham was not completed until 1872 and it was not until after the races, in 1906, that the need for the reversal of East Coast trains at Newcastle ceased.

The amalgamation that brought the North Eastern Railway into being took place in 1854 after the demise of Hudson. The major constituents were the original Hudson company, the York & North Midland, along with the Leeds Northern, and the York, Newcastle & Berwick Railway which had been formed by incorporation in 1847. In 1855 the Octuple Agreement, the name given to the traffic pooling agreement which had been forced upon the Great Northern Railway back in 1850, came to an end and as it did so new traffic arrangements between the East Coast railways were made on more favourable terms. This is also the point at which the King's Cross/East Coast route became the established route, that is, it no longer shared the 'East Coast' appellation with the Euston, Rugby, Derby, Normanton, York route.

The first locomotive engineer to the newly amalgamated North Eastern Railway was Edward Fletcher, and on his appointment he inherited one of the most diverse and ragtag fleets of locomotives it is possible to imagine; the first of his tasks was to try to bring some semblance of order and standardization. The problems of standardization were further bedevilled by the fact that there were workshops at Holbeck, Darlington (after 1862 and the amalgamation of the Stockton & Darlington), York and Gateshead. Despite a reign lasting twenty-eight years, Fletcher did not completely succeed in standardizing the motive power fleet, but at least he had recognized the need to attempt it.

The progress of the North Eastern was only marginally less successful than that of the London & North Western and despite the latter's greater size, it was the North Eastern which paid the higher dividends, particularly in the late 1860s and early part of the 1870s. One reason why it is possible to argue that the races of 1895 were a high-water mark is that by that time the dividend percentages being paid on all railway shares were in decline.

The rosy outlook that seemed to beckon the North Eastern in the early 1870s was not entirely fulfilled, and one of the principal causes of the failure to make further improvements was the onset of a general nationwide depression. The depression led to falling prices, falling demand, labour unrest and bankruptcies, especially in the coal and iron industries of north-east England. The high point of 1873 became the low of 1879. Another reason for a decline in revenues had been the decision in 1875, by the Midland Railway, to abolish second class, carry third class on all services and reduce first-class fares to only 50 per cent more than third. The fares reductions by the Midland were followed within the year by the opening of its route to Scotland via the Settle/Carlisle line and the fallout from these events effectively forced the other 'London to the North' companies to follow suit and make alterations to their own fares structures.

The discussion of the history of the competitors has, thus far, been more concerned with the East Coast companies – the North British, North Eastern and Great Northern Railways. At this point there needs to be some mention of the background of the two West Coast partners – the London & North Western and the Caledonian.

Captain Mark Huish, the general manager who had been so influential in the early dealings of the London & North Western, was pushed to resign in 1858. The man who had been chairman for many years and was most responsible for the creation of the Railway Clearing House, George Carr Glyn, a banker, had been replaced in 1853 by the Marquis of Chandos, later the Duke of Buckingham. Chandos was followed by the short-lived appointment of another of the early supporters, Admiral Moorsom. Moorsom had been involved with the London & North Western for many years and it was death that made his term of office short, rather than any failings as a leader. Moorsom was replaced by Richard Moon in 1861.

It was from Moon's appointment onward that the growth in power and prosperity of the London & North Western company continued almost unabated for more than two decades. Richard Moon himself is repeatedly characterized as being very tight-fisted and is generally credited with producing drastic reductions in operating costs. In the first ten years of Moon's reign the London & North Western grew, chiefly by amalgamation, from 929 miles to 1,506 miles, and despite this growth in size and complexity economies were made, though their nature is often strangely contradictory. The expense of fitting improved brake systems on locomotives and coaches was resisted on cost grounds. However, the widespread installation of the Saxby and Farmer interlocking system went ahead because the capital cost could be recouped through the use of fewer signalmen, with a consequent reduction in operating costs. However, even this was not enough for Moon and by 1873 he had cut out the Saxby and Farmer contract and set the railway's own workshops at Crewe to the task of making signalling equipment under the appointment of an engineer, responsible to the chief mechanical engineer. One interesting note on the development of signalling was that F.W. Webb, chief mechanical engineer to the London & North Western in 1873, is credited as being among the first to develop the pressed steel signal arm.

Moon, though, was more than a cost-cutting skinflint, he had the ability to spot the right man for a job and had his own motto for them to live up to on their appointment:

Remember, first, that you are a gentleman; remember, next, that you are a North Western officer, and that whatever you promise you must perform – therefore, be careful what you promise, but having promised it, take care that you perform it.

Nock, *North Western*, p. 96

Moon is credited with the foresight that put Ramsbottom in charge at Crewe Works and, following McConnell's 'engineered' resignation from the post of chief mechanical engineer for the southern division of the London & North Western at Wolverton, Ramsbottom was put in sole charge of the locomotive department for the whole of the London & North Western. The influence of Ramsbottom and importance of the workshops at Crewe should not be underestimated, especially when one considers the number of locomotive engineers who served their apprenticeships there. The designer of the locomotives which hauled the race trains on the North Eastern Railway, Worsdell, served his time at Crewe, and the famous Great Northern Railway engineer, Ivatt, trained at Crewe. Perhaps most famous of all was another Crewe apprentice, Sir Nigel Gresley.

Between his appointment in 1857 and his retirement in 1871, Ramsbottom presided over a fall in locomotive operating expenses from marginally under 5*d* per mile to 3*d* per mile, no mean achievement when one considers the growing payloads and an expanding network. Ramsbottom was succeeded by the able but erratic Francis William Webb, another London & North Western man with something of a 'reputation' and arguably the only man on the railway during the period who could and did stand up to Richard Moon. Webb's reign at Crewe, like that of of his predecessor Ramsbottom, was marked by a high degree of standardization with large numbers of locomotives being built in only a small number of classes; for example some eight hundred of the Ramsbottom 'DX' class 0–6–0 goods engines were built. However, unlike Ramsbottom, who had proved his worth as an engineer before joining the London & North Western, Webb had been an apprentice at Crewe and was recruited back into London & North Western service from the Bolton Iron and Steel Works where he had been manager since 1866. (Ramsbottom had patented designs for a double-valve regulator, safety valves, the split piston–ring and the displacement lubricator to his credit; the split piston–ring having applications far beyond the confines of railway locomotive engineering.)

The practices of standardized forms of construction carried on at Crewe and the drive for reductions in operating cost demanded by Euston, are the principal trends in company policy and practice on the London & North Western during the Moon chairmanship. In purely operational terms the London & North Western was one of the first to recognize the losses caused by delay and as a result was one of the first railways, if not the first railway, to begin using the flyover and its corollary the burrowing junction or underpass, in preference to the 'on the level' junctions with their inbuilt delay. Another feature of Crewe practice was what today would be called 'build quality', that is they ensured that products built in the works were produced to the highest standards, which translated into longevity in service and lower maintenance costs.

*Considering the criticisms levelled at the designer of this locomotive, F.W. Webb, it is perhaps remarkable that No. 1054 is still in active service 107 years after construction in 1888. The coach that No. 1054 is pulling is older still; having been built for the Stockton & Darlington Railway, it became the North Eastern Railway's inspection saloon in 1884, for use by the locomotive superintendent and was undoubtedly used by both the Worsdells and Vincent Raven.*

The range and diversity of the standardized products created by the workshops at Crewe were in contrast to much of what was then current railway engineering practice. The policies of economy emanating from Euston and carried out at Crewe not only helped to carry forward the cause of standardization, they also played a part in the decisions that led to Crewe having its own steelworks, which has been described as the first commercial steel-making plant in the world and following its enlargement was the first to roll rails in 60 ft lengths – a first which lasted until after Grouping in 1923.

Traditions and practices started by Ramsbottom were continued by Webb and it was Webb's locomotives, despite many and often justified criticisms of the man's engineering abilities, which carried the London & North Western's colours into the races. On the management side the economies demanded by Moon as chairman were backed up by the organizational achievements of George Findlay. Findlay, the general manager, believed in thorough training, and some very famous names in railway management came from the Findlay school. Perhaps the best known of those pupils were Frederick Harrison, Frank Ree and Robert Turnbull, who like Findlay all received knighthoods for their services to the railway industry.

Findlay's organizational ability, which has already been commented upon, was strengthened by his recognition of the commercial benefits to be derived from the advocacy of fair pay and conditions:

> Every man should be fairly remunerated for his labour, and should be, as far as it lies with the management to make him so, a cheerful and contented servant. A discontented man makes a bad servant, for his mind is often preoccupied by his own real or fancied grievances when it should be concentrated on his employer's business.
>
> Nock, *North Western*, p. 90

However, Findlay's enlightened attitude to pay and conditions did not extend to the trade union movement:

> Might as well have trade unionism in Her Majesty's Army as to have it in railway service.
>
> *Royal Commission on Labour*, British Parliamentary Papers (BBP), vol. 33 (1893/4)

The London & North Western's seemingly enlightened attitudes to staff, trade unionists excepted, was not universal in the railway business and it is fair to say that the physical construction of the railways was achieved by men, and to an extent by women, in the most atrocious conditions of hardship and privation it is possible to imagine. The life of the navvy was in every sense nasty, brutish and short. Employees of the London & North Western, on the other hand, benefited not only from fair pay policies, but from company hospitals, libraries, housing, even fresh water supplies. This latter may not seem a great matter today, but in the mid-nineteenth century it was something of a luxury, or even a life enhancer as this quote from a report on the sanitary conditions of the labouring population in 1842 indicates:

> [They] rise early, before daylight in winter time, to go to their work; they toil hard, and they return to their homes late at night. It is a serious inconvenience, as well as discomfort to them to have to fetch water at a distance out-of-doors, from the pump or the river on every occasion that it may be wanted, whether it may be in cold, in rain or in snow.
>
> *Report on the Sanitary Condition of the Labouring Population*, 1842, p. 70, from Gregg, *Social and Economic History*, p. 196

The London & North Western's partner in operating the services to Scotland was the Caledonian. The cooperation between the two companies began with the Caledonian's initial promotion and by 1848 the two were able to offer direct railway services between Euston and Glasgow, with connections to Edinburgh. In 1848 the advantage enjoyed by the West Coast route lay in passengers not having to detrain and the fact that the direct East Coast route was not yet opened throughout – advantages which had only a few years to run.

Like the London & North Western and the rest of the competing companies, the Caledonian grew by amalgamation, but its growth and prosperity was not without periods of some anxiety. The Caledonian Bill passed through parliament at the height of the Mania of 1845, receiving the Royal Assent in July of that year. Obtaining the Royal Assent cost the promoters £75,000 in legal and parliamentary fees, which is a large sum for the time, though much less than the amount it cost the London & York. An interesting comparison can be found in the costs for the building of Carlisle's famous Citadel station, which opened in 1848 at a total cost of £155,689, of which the Caledonian paid £51,367, with the remainder being paid by the Lancaster & Carlisle, or London & North Western as it incorporated the former.

The Caledonian began its operations with Hope-Johnstone, the staunchest of the line's original promoters, as chairman and by August 1847 the contractor Thomas Brassey had 20,000 men at work on the construction. The Carlisle–Beattock section was brought into operation the same year. This early success was not sustained and by 1849 inexperienced management had led the company to the brink of ruin. Much of the funding for the Caledonian had come from England, and when it became apparent that all was not well a group of leading shareholders formed themselves into the London Central Committee of Caledonian Shareholders. Led by Captain E. Plunkett, the committee sent out a circular to all shareholders expressing their concerns, and the Caledonian's share price slumped on the stock exchange.

During the unsettled period between 1848 and 1850 the Caledonian was involved in disputes with the Newcastle & Carlisle Railway over the leasing of the Maryport & Carlisle Railway and also with the Glasgow & South Western. The principal causes of the dispute with the Glasgow & South Western were the running powers over the Caledonian from Gretna to Carlisle and the use of Carlisle Citadel station. The dispute was principally financial: the Caledonian charged £5,000 per annum for the running powers, £1,000 for the use of Citadel station, plus a contribution to the running costs. The Glasgow & South Western objected, claiming the sums were too large.

The rescue of the Caledonian's fortunes came about through the actions of Plunkett and the committee and also through the rather remarkable actions of a millionaire industrialist called James Baird, who is reported as simply having walked into the Caledonian's offices and purchased a major holding in the company. Both Baird and Plunkett joined the board and from this rather close call with bankruptcy the Caledonian went on to become Scotland's 'Premier Line'. The Caledonian had, at this early stage of its existence, a rather unusual by-law: there was to be no smoking on trains or in stations, a law that would seem more in keeping with the mores of current society. Another area of company practice, which (unlike the smoking) would seem out of place today, was the running of trains on a Sunday and in Scotland in particular this was a major debate.

The association between the Caledonian and the companies which became the London & North Western ran to much more than financial support. Much of the Caledonian's initial route and its eventual main line through to Aberdeen was surveyed and the contracts let by Joseph Locke, chief engineer of the Grand Junction at the time. Robert Sinclair, a pupil of Robert Stephenson from the London & Birmingham days, became at first general manager of the Glasgow, Paisley & Greenock Railway (a line absorbed by the Caledonian), later becoming locomotive superintendent and then general manager of the Caledonian from 1852 to 1856. Another Grand Junction man heavily involved with the early years of the Caledonian was the former Edge Hill Works manager, Alexander Allan, whose Crewe-type locomotives formed the backbone of the early Caledonian motive power. Allan had moved from chief foreman at Crewe to the post of locomotive superintendent on the Scottish Central Railway; after this line was absorbed by the Caledonian Allan was made locomotive superintendent to the Caledonian.

The Caledonian, unlike its partner to the south, was quite content to buy in locomotives from outside manufacturers, and the Vulcan Foundry, Nielson's and the North British Locomotive Company all at one time or other supplied locomotives for the Caledonian. However, despite the use of contractors, in 1856 the railway appointed Benjamin Conner to the post of locomotive superintendent and he began to improve and enlarge the Caledonian's own workshops at St Rollox. The actions of individual officers within an organization could and did differ from what might be termed company policy; one such case involved Conner and Patrick Stirling. The Caledonian and the Glasgow & South Western fought like cat and dog for trade, territory and company honour, yet Conner invited Stirling, who at the time was locomotive engineer to the Glasgow & South Western, to visit St Rollox to inspect the new 8 ft 'single' he had constructed. There are suggestions that it is from this that Stirling developed his own 'singles' which gave such reliable if not spectacular service on the Great Northern, especially in the races.

By the mid-1860s the Caledonian was also battling it out with the North British, particularly as the North British had amalgamated the Edinburgh & Glasgow Railway and somewhat oddly the Monklands & Kirkintilloch Railway – a small part of which was actually a part of the Caledonian route to Aberdeen. The constant sparring between these three Scottish railway companies extended beyond the immediate confines of the track and manifested itself in the battle for supremacy on the Clyde Steamer services. The Caledonian vied with the North British and the Glasgow & South Western to provide the best steamer connection services – with the Caledonian even going so far as to build new lines and improve and extend piers, eventually launching its own boats and employing the most audacious of the steamer captains to run its services – the competition on water being every bit as fierce as that on land, and in the 1890s racing to gain the best berths was common practice among the steamer skippers.

The 1860s saw the rebuilding of Aberdeen station and the Caledonian embarked upon an expansion of the port facilities at Grangemouth, chiefly as a centre for coal exports to Russia and Europe. Railway growth and expansion in

Britain enjoyed a little boom period from the end of the 1850s up to the mid-1860s. In Scotland the boom involved not only the expansion of facilities, but was also manifest in the amalgamations of 1865–6 which, as has been mentioned, involved both the Caledonian and the North British.

Each of the five competing companies has its own unique history, but they all share in a larger and more complex history, that of the industrial society and capitalism. The years of growing prosperity in Britain from the triumphal Great Exhibition of 1851 enter into a decline in the early 1870s and this decline is not simply in production and monetary terms, but is also manifest in the form of quality of the finished goods and of the economics of producing them. Britain's situation can be seen in microcosm in the relationships surrounding the birth of the Great Northern Railway; coming later to the railway business the Great Northern was able to gain from the experiences of the competition and avoid some of their more obvious mistakes. The British, having been first in the industrial revolution field, found the opposition 'coming up on the rails', to coin a phrase. Britain was exporting rail to America and locomotives, navvies and engineers to France, to name but two countries, but by the 1870s these forms of export were starting to decline and by the 1880s had almost ceased. Having learned from the British, the Germans, French, Belgians and Americans were able to institute the most modern and up-to-date techniques, especially in iron and steel production and the system of factory mechanization, resulting in their goods being cheaper to produce and of better standards of manufacture.

These changes in economic fortunes affected all the competing companies, though not all in the same way or at the same time. Changes in the iron and steel trade caused much greater difficulties for the North Eastern than for the Caledonian, and the North British had greater difficulties with trade union activity than the London & North Western. There were relatively few strikes in the railway industry itself, but strikes by those involved in mining (both coal and iron ores) had quite noticeable impacts upon railway finances. The one major rail strike in the 1870s, that by enginemen of the North Eastern Railway, saw the strikers defeated by the employment of blackleg labour with only a hundred or so of the more than a thousand strikers retaining their jobs.

The measure of the competitors has numerous yardsticks. Profits generated, dividends paid, value of assets or market share, brand loyalty, credit rating, quality of management – all generated valuable information about the state of corporate health, in much the same way as a general medical examination will reveal the health or not of the patient. From a racing point of view the strengths of the competitors in economic terms was of less importance than the state of the permanent way, the quality of the signalling system, the power outputs and reliability of the locomotives, and the determination and motivation of staff, which were obviously of far greater importance than the share price or asset value, though it is entirely possible that these latter issues came into consideration when deciding whether to race or not.

All the racing companies grew through amalgamation, they all built new and joint lines, they all improved their routes through the addition of feeder branch lines and new handling facilities, new stations, warehouses, freight yards, and doubling and quadrupling of tracks with better ballasting for smoother travel and higher speeds – though there were still single line sections on parts of the North British's section of the race route. There is another dimension to consider in assessing the effects of so much intense activity, and that is the tendency to champion one party or one set of parameters to the detriment of the rest. In the case of the races there are those who even today champion the East Coast or the Great Northern, while others argue that the Caledonian held the highest operating standards. Personal tastes and peccadillos are unlikely to be swayed by figures of pounds per mile coal consumption or the dividend earnings, when compared with such transports of delight as the Stirling 8 ft 'singles' or the handsome Drummond 4–4–0s of the Caledonian with their striking blue paintwork.

There was an air of incestuousness in the early railway industry, noticeable on several levels. The interchange of management and engineering staff, the following in father's footsteps, promotional transfers from one company to another, the relationship between promoters, board members, contractors and leading shareholders, many of whom had crossover holdings, and membership on more than one Board of Directors, or of either Houses of Parliament. Contractors not only built lines, in recessions they promoted and financed lines, so as to keep their own plant and organizations intact. Almost every conceivable form of contractual arrangement existed between railway companies and the individuals who ran, financed and built them. Thomas Brassey took mortgages on behalf of the Great Northern Railway in lieu of cash payment, and payment of contractors by giving them shares in lieu was a relatively common practice. For years the Great Western had all trains stopping at Swindon, the reason being that having run short of funds to complete the station the contractors agreed to finish the job in exchange for the concession on the refreshment rooms.

Mountfield sums up the situation quite succinctly:

> The whole business was so novel, so huge and so complicated that the administrative machinery to organise it simply did not exist and had to be invented, usually by men in a hurry and often lacking moral scruples, as they went along.
>
> Mountfield, *The Railway Barons*, p. 8

The dividend percentages, paid by the companies involved in the racing, ranged from the solid consistency of the London & North Western which, from 1865 to 1914 paid between 5⅜ per cent and 7¾ per cent with the average being in excess of 6 per cent, to the erratic performance of the North British which had a high of only 4½ per cent and a great many years where dividends were nil or only fractions of a per cent. The highest dividends of the competing companies were those of the North Eastern which had a high of 9¼ per cent in 1873 and a low of 4⅞ per cent in 1892, the average for the 1856–1914 period being around 6½ per cent. The Caledonian never quite achieved the stable consistency of the North Eastern or London & North Western, but it was the most consistent of the Scottish lines, with a high of 8 per cent in 1865 followed by a low of 2 per cent in

1868. However, in broad terms the Caledonian paid around 4 per cent to 4½ per cent and in Scotland only the Glasgow & South Western offered similar rates of return. Like the North Eastern, the Great Northern paid its highest dividend, 7¼ per cent, in 1873 with its lowest, 3 per cent, in 1893. However, the Great Northern dividends had a slow but almost continuous decline from 1873 onwards.

Dividend earnings from all British railway companies showed some degree of decline from the 1880s onward, though in some cases the decline was much more marked than in others. From its high in 1873 the Great Northern showed a 50 per cent decline over the next two decades, while during the same period the London & North Western showed a drop of less than 25 per cent, and the North Eastern dividends slipped by around a third. The North British showed some movement against the general trend with its best dividends being paid between 1882 and 1888. However, these seven years were the highlight of the North British's performance and from 1889 dividends were declining and only in 1902/3 did they exceed 2 per cent with nil dividends in 1891 and again in the race year. The Caledonian's share dividends remained reasonably consistent, though here again the highest dividends were in the years 1866 and 1876/7.

Size and overall market share is not always a guarantee of the highest rates of interest, and during the periods under discussion the Taff Vale Railway posted dividends of between 15 per cent and 17½ per cent, while the Maryport & Carlisle paid between 11 per cent and 13 per cent for the six years 1870 to 1875, and if one discounts 1879, when 8¾ per cent was paid, not less than 10½ per cent was paid from 1870 to 1882.

If the dividend percentage figures of the competing companies represented the real nature of the strength of the companies then it would be possible to say that the front runners were the North Eastern and London & North Western, with the Great Northern just ahead of the Caledonian and the North British a long way adrift in fifth place. These share dividend indicators, however, are only part of the picture and to obtain a more accurate appraisal more practical matters must be given due and fair consideration, for example the single tracking of part of the North British's route from Edinburgh to Aberdeen.

The nature and quality of the total route and its engineering standard, in relation to such advances as the provision of water troughs, allowing water to be collected while on the move, ruling gradients, track alignment and the strength and quality of rail in use, the amount and severity of curves, the quality of signalling equipment, and even track layouts at important stations and junctions all had a direct influence on the outcome of the races and have relevance to the actual strengths and weaknesses of the competitors, not just in race terms but in their respective positions within the history of the British railway network. Similarly the locomotives and coaching-stock played more important roles in a race than the blend of tea served in the buffet car or the price of the shares on the stock market, and the influences of these more practical issues will be discussed later.

## Chapter Two

# A BRIDGE TOO FAR

When the green flag waved and the whistles blew for the 'off' in July 1895, Victoria had reigned for over fifty years, the Empire was a source of vast reserves of raw materials, a 'captive' market existed for British-made goods and services and the twentieth century was about to dawn. British-built shipping was carrying British-built manufactures and British railways were arteries of the nation's distribution network along which these vast tonnages flowed from port to factory, to shop, to table. To paraphrase a slogan of the road haulage industry: 'If you got it, it came by train.' In 1895 the figures for miles of line open and goods and passengers carried spoke for themselves: 21,174 miles of line open for traffic, as compared with 10,433 in 1860, 929,770,909 passengers carried – exclusive of season ticket holders, 334,929,513 tons of freight carried. However, large though these numbers seem, there were problems; the percentage of working expenditure to gross receipts was worsening. In 1860 the figure was 47 per cent; this had slipped to 53 per cent by 1885 and had been eroded further to 56 per cent by 1895. By the turn of the century it was 62 per cent and, despite rising numbers of passengers and freight tonnages, net receipts to paid up capital also fell from 4.19 per cent in 1860 and 4.74 per cent in 1872 to 3.80 per cent in the race year and 3.41 per cent in 1900.

A far-sighted Victorian businessman might have seen even further troubles on the horizon for the railways. The birth of the internal combustion engine, the diesel engine and the beginnings of the telephone system were all new businesses on the agenda in 1895. The first of many London Motor Exhibitions took place in 1895, Dunlop had already patented the pneumatic tyre and London and several Continental cities had rudimentary telephone systems. Paris had been linked with Brussels and Marseilles in 1889, and in 1891 Paris and London were connected by telephone. Perhaps most significantly of all, the Lord Mayor of London inaugurated the London telephone system on 12 June 1895. Of all the advances in the first half of the twentieth century none would do more to bring about the demise of the railway network than this particular clutch of new technologies. The telegraph, so important to the control of the railway network and until this point the only really efficient method of long-distance communication, was losing its monopoly at the very moment the races were being run. What had been the first practical use of electricity back in the late 1830s was now becoming old technology.

The nineteenth century was an age of grand schemes: the Suez Canal, and Cecil Rhodes and his Cape to Cairo Railway. It was also an age of exhibitions, a trend started by the Great Exhibition of 1851, itself an event closely allied to the railways. In 1880s Britain the exhibition was an important form of public entertainment – for example there was an Inventions Exhibition in London in 1885 and other large-scale public exhibitions took place, in Manchester in 1887, in Edinburgh in 1890, while on the other side of the Atlantic, Chicago held its 'Worlds Fair' in 1893. Such events provided custom for the railways but they also provided the public with examples of ways in which technological innovation was changing pre-existing ideas across a range of products, with transport and communications being in the van.

Leaving aside, for now, the technological threats to railway supremacy as both carrier and communicator, in 1888 a more prosaic issue was occupying the management teams of the East and West Coast rivals. The age-old struggle for traffic was back on the agenda, if indeed it ever left it. Prior to the races of 1895 there was, in 1888, another series of 'accelerations' based on the timings of the services to Edinburgh. However, although the contest was to reach Edinburgh first, an important element in the motivation of the West Coast partners was the looming prospect of the opening of the Forth Bridge, and the subsequent shortening of the East Coast route to the far north of Scotland, as these comments from the *Pall Mall Gazette* acknowledge:

> The main cause confronts us when we see those three stupendous towers of steel which loom above the horizon of Edinburgh. When the Forth Bridge is finished the North Western and Caledonian will have to struggle hard if they wish to retain much of the traffic to Dundee or Aberdeen, and may possibly be robbed of some of that to Inverness.

Nock, Railway Race to the North, p. 62

The accelerations of 1888 are an echo, both of the deliberately provocative events of 1857 when the Great Northern and the Manchester, Sheffield & Lincoln ran a joint service to Manchester, in direct competition with the London & North Western, and of those of 1869 when the East Coast partners announced their new 8 p.m. service to Edinburgh, to which the West Coast answer was its own 8 p.m. service. Late in 1887 the East Coast companies announced that the 10 a.m. 'Flying Scotsman' service would carry third–class passengers. The West Coast chose to reply not by a fares reduction or classes carried alteration of its own, but by an acceleration, from 2 June 1888, of its 10 a.m. 'Scotch Express'. The decision was a well-kept secret and its implementation left until as late as possible to make it difficult for the East Coast to reciprocate. In the event, two weeks went by before the East Coast announced accelerations of its own, which would take place as from 1 July.

Making substantial changes to timetables is not an easy matter and one can imagine the fevered activity needed to effect the complex alterations in so short a period. The retiming of passing points, the printing and issuing of amended timings to signalmen along the entire route and new connecting services to coordinate, all come into play in any changes in running times. Creating this situation at the beginning of the heavy summer season traffic, as the West Coast companies did, made the situation even more complicated. The West Coast partners, having started the accelerations, felt that they had to respond to the East Coast retiming due to come into effect from 1 July, though now their decision to leave matters until the beginning of the summer services rebounded on them.

The initial reduction by the West Coast amounted to 1 hour from their 10 hour schedule; the East Coast response was to cut 30 minutes from their 9 hour schedule which, in turn, was matched by the West Coast team. The East Coast then went for another 30 minute reduction and again the West Coast matched them. In the last days of the accelerations, matters had progressed to the point where, as Nock states:

> . . . there is no doubt that racing fever had taken complete hold of the West Coast companies. In countering the final East Coast acceleration of August 14th they threw caution to the winds, and without the flicker of an eyelid ran their train as far ahead of time as their engines could take it.
>
> Nock, *Railway Race to the North*, p. 46

Like the races of 1895, those of 1888 went on for a period of weeks rather than being a one-off event. However, in his *Railway Race to the North*, Nock appears to offer a conflict of interpretation. After detailing the levels of rivalry and the attempted cloak and dagger secrecy with which the races were conducted, and the fact that the events took place during that period which is generally referred to as the 'silly season', that is when parliament is in summer recess, Nock contends that this inevitably led to the interest of the press, an interest which, he states, was not entirely appreciated by the competitors.

> Publicity for this speed contest was the last thing the leading railways wanted; for against the sensationally written-up glamour of acceleration there was inevitably a good deal of scaremongering among the fainthearts.
>
> Nock, *Railway Race to the North*, p. 40

The question here is not whether it was right to race, especially when carrying large numbers of people, many of whom would have been unaware that they were participants in a contest, but is Nock correct in his assertion that the railways did not want the glare of publicity? Nock offers no tangible evidence that the railways did not want publicity and, after all, what are a few sad letters to the editor when compared with, 'sensationally written-up glamour'?

The whole exercise can be seen not only as an attempt to counteract the threat posed by the Forth Bridge, but as one designed to lure passengers by appealing to their desires for a fast service. That the public possessed such a desire had been evidenced by their choices of services during the fare wars of 1856, referred to in chapter one. Attempting to gain trade by faster services rather than cheaper fares, is tantamount to admitting that rapidity is the selling point and therefore publicizing this aspect was precisely what the railway wanted. That the East Coast responded by accelerating their own services rather than offering even lower fares is in part an admission that speed was a factor in the passengers' choice of route and service.

The West Coast knew that the faster services would attract press attention, unless they were naïve in the extreme, and that this attention would inevitably concentrate on the speed – if not, why choose this method to combat the East Coast's carriage of third-class passengers on the prime day service train, namely the 10 a.m. ex-King's Cross? The admission of third-class passengers to one of its fastest services was in itself a recognition that the travelling public wants to travel by the faster services. Commenting on the lives of the great engineers, Nock quotes that popular and well-loved Victorian engineer Isambard Kingdom Brunel:

> I shall not attempt to argue with those who consider any increase in speed unnecessary. The public will always prefer that conveyance which is the most perfect and speed within reasonable limits, is a material ingredient in perfection of travelling.

> Nock, *The Railway Engineers*, p. 251

In *Railway Race to the North*, Nock describes how three men, W.M. Acworth, Norman D. Macdonald and Revd W.J. Scott, had gained privileged access to operational information through their acquaintance with the senior officers of the competing companies and he goes on to say of them that they were,

> the three men who did more than anyone else to arouse the interest and enthusiasm of newspaper editors, and so to bring the affair prominently before the public . . .

> Nock, *Railway Race to the North*, pp. 39, 40

These remarks would seem to indicate that the companies not only chose to race their trains, but that they had every intention of so doing and that they fully intended that this should be publicized. Why else would they have briefed the correspondents Acworth et al.?

The West Coast partnership had ample time in which to contemplate its reaction to the East Coast's decision to carry third-class passengers on the 10 a.m. ex-King's Cross, thus it would seem unlikely that the choice to accelerate the services was a hasty or unconsidered judgement. Given the history of the rivalry between the London & North Western and the Great Northern in particular, the management at Euston can have been in little doubt as to how the East Coast team would react and there is every likelihood that they fully expected the reply they received, though whether they anticipated its swiftness is another matter.

Once the gauntlet had been picked up, the West Coast companies were not about to capitulate and a special committee of directors was set up to monitor and coordinate the events. It was this committee that decided to match the 8 hour schedule put in place by the East Coast partners, and they also chose to do this commencing on Monday 6 August, which in 1888 was Bank Holiday Monday.

This was accomplished a mere five days after the revised East Coast times of 1 August and only nine days after they had set up their own 8½ hour timings. For a week the two routes both completed the journey in 8 hours, then the East Coast team announced that from 14 August they would complete the journey in 7 hours 45 minutes.

The reaction of the West Coast was immediate. On 13 August they ran their train into Edinburgh at 5.38 p.m., 7 hours 38 minutes after departure from Euston, knocking 7 minutes off the freshly announced East Coast service timing. The upshot of this event was that both sides met the next day and agreed that no new accelerations would be made and that for the rest of the month the East Coast would run the distance in 7¾ hours and the West Coast in 8 hours. Despite the agreement, on 31 August the East Coast chose to run as fast as possible to Edinburgh, and in doing so managed to beat the West Coast's average speed of 52.3 m.p.h. for the very fast journey put in on 13 August, by posting an average 52.7 m.p.h. themselves. A difference of 0.4 m.p.h. over a journey of almost 400 miles was a very close call.

The comparisons with the speeds of January 1888 and those of the journeys on 13 and 31 August are quite marked. The highest average speed in January on the London & North Western/Caledonian route was 47.3 m.p.h. over the Euston–Rugby section. In June this had risen to a new high of 51.5 m.p.h. on the Rugby–Crewe stretch, and on the run of 13 August it had risen again to 57.4 m.p.h., and this was over the Carlisle–Edinburgh portion of the route, with both Beattock and Cobbinshaw banks to contend with. The corresponding East Coast figures are 49.6 m.p.h. between Grantham and York in June 1888, 51.6 m.p.h. over the same section in July and no less than 59.4 m.p.h. over the York–Newcastle stretch on the run of 31 August. Chapter five details locomotive performances, covering the races of 1888 and 1895, and more recent performances from the Grouping era and after are discussed in chapter six.

The bout of midsummer madness was replaced in September with a reversion, by both parties, to the timings in force in July, the West Coast taking 8½ hours, with the East Coast taking 15 minutes less. Though not as rapid as the fastest of the race timings the new times were a significant saving on those of late 1887 to early 1888 when the West Coast schedule was 10 hours and the East Coast's was 9 hours.

There can be little doubt that both management groups were participating in a battle for business using whatever means they had at their disposal. The class, the cost, the speed and the comfort of travel were all used by railway managements to boost trade, as were excursions – whole, half-day or evening. Trains to races, football matches, the seaside or country, every conceivable manner of promoting travel by rail was explored and promoting faster services to a popular holiday destination such as Scotland was almost certain to generate new trade, particularly as the whole event was being played out on the pages of the daily papers during the height of the holiday season. Another point which Nock misses is that the newspaper coverage amounted to free advertising, some of it extremely flattering publicity.

The racing of 1888 can viewed as being a preamble to the races of 1895. However, despite there being only a seven-year gap, the two contests were waged by quite different personnel. On the West Coast side the powerful influence of Richard Moon as chairman came to an end in 1891 and that of George Findlay as general manager in 1892. Findlay was replaced in 1893 by Frederick Harrison, a man Nock refers to as 'very definitely the commander-in-chief' (Nock, *Railway Race to the North*, p. 66).

There had been changes too among the East Coast partners. On the North Eastern Railway Henry Tennant retired as general manager in 1892 to be replaced by George Stegman Gibb, and in the locomotive department Wilson Worsdell replaced his brother Thomas. These changes on both the North Eastern and the London & North Western had several consequences for the events of 1895, in relation to company policy on the one hand and locomotive design on the other.

At the time of the Races to the North, second and third generation railwaymen were taking the reins in all departments. These were men who for the most part had spent almost all their working lives in the railway industry and many with fathers and grandfathers, uncles and cousins having done so before them or who were doing so along side them. George S. Gibb, who was general manager of the North Eastern when the 1895 races were held, had been the railway's solicitor from 1882; his father was at one time chief engineer to the Great North of Scotland Railway and in cooperation with his father, Stegman Gibb's grandfather had owned the firm that built the bridge over the River Wear, opened in 1838 as part of what was then the Durham Junction Railway.

The Pease family, who were among the chief promoters of the Stockton & Darlington Railway, were also significant in their influence. They had four generations with sixteen different family members on the board of the North Eastern Railway. From its formation in 1854 to its amalgamation into the London & North Eastern Railway at the Grouping of 1923, there was a Pease involved in the boardroom activity. Joseph Whitwell Pease, a director in 1863, became deputy chairman in 1888 and chairman in 1895. J.W. Pease was forced to resign his chairmanship in 1902, following a banking scandal in which the private bank he owned went bankrupt owing the sum of £125,000 to the North Eastern. Pease, like many other railway company directors and entrepreneurs, was also an MP, representing South Durham for twenty years between 1865 and 1885.

These forms of family connections were not isolated occurrences and railway dynasties were not confined to the upper echelons, for the same kind of kinship relations can be found among footplate crews, signalmen and station staff. Clerical grades were no different, in fact securing a clerical post was frequently dependent upon personal recommendation or some associated form of patronage. In the very early years railway company directors often had quite specific rights in the allocation of employment within the company, frequently being provided with set numbers of vacancies which they could fill with their own protégés.

Many chairmen and their chief executives in the Victorian railway companies were either members of the Lords or received knighthoods for their services to the state and the railway industry, though there were those whose behaviour can be interpreted as less than chivalrous. Sir Edward Watkin, knighted for his services to the State in overseeing the construction of Grand Trunk Railway in Canada, was chairman of the Manchester, Sheffield & Lincoln Railway (often rudely

*Sir George Gibb, general manager of the North Eastern Railway. (National Railway Museum)*

referred to as the 'Money Sunk and Lost Railway'), a post he held simultaneously with one as chairman of the board on the South Eastern & Chatham. If this was not enough, Watkin was also a board member with the Metropolitan Railway and, in addition to his considerable railway interests, at various times Watkin was MP for Hythe, for Yarmouth and for Stockport. Despite holding such high office and being an MP, the *Dictionary of Business Biography* says of him:

> Everywhere he went, controversy and acrimony reigned, fuelled by a blunt and aggressive personality which was intolerant of criticism.
>
> *Dictionary of Business Biography*, vol. 5, S–Z, p. 622

Watkin first became involved with the railways in 1845 when he was appointed to the post of secretary to the Trent Valley Railway, later to become a part of the London & North Western. Watkin remained with the London & North Western until 1854 when he created a stir by taking his considerable knowledge of the workings of the London & North Western to the Manchester, Sheffield & Lincoln. For an encore he left the Manchester, Sheffield & Lincoln in the middle of negotiating a take-over of the company by the Great Northern, to take up the post of advisor on the construction of the Grand Trunk of Canada. It was on his return to Britain, after the sojourn in Canada, that he held two posts as chairman – from 1864 he returned to the Manchester, Sheffield & Lincoln and in 1866 he took the chair on the South Eastern & Chatham. Watkin remained in office until 1894 when he resigned from both his chairmanships.

Though no longer directly involved in the boardroom of the London & North Western at the time of the racing, Watkin was an important and influential figure in British railway management and as such, through various committee and organizational meetings, was closely associated with those directors and officers who were involved in the 'accelerations'. It is perhaps less than coincidental that one of the railways most criticized by Colonel Yolland of the Railway Inspectorate for their failure to act on his recommendations on braking systems was the Manchester, Sheffield & Lincoln, another was its one-time collaborator, the Great Northern.

During the racing era King's Cross, home of the Great Northern, was the fiefdom of another lifelong railwayman who was also knighted for his services. Sir Henry Oakley began and ended his railway career with the Great Northern, joining the company in 1850, after having spent a brief period as a House of Commons clerk, during which time he became familiar with the Great Northern in its two-year battle to gain parliamentary approval. Oakley was appointed to the post of company secretary in 1854, after he discovered the frauds of Leo Redpath and, in 1870, he succeeded the guileless but passenger-friendly Seymour Clarke as general manager.

In length of service, Oakley was one of the most senior of the officers in charge during the races. The changes in personnel on the London & North Western, referred to earlier, were matched almost to a man on the North Eastern Railway and on the Great Northern. On the North Eastern, in addition to the changes of general manager and locomotive superintendent, the chairmanship changed hands in 1895 following the death in 1894 of John Dent Dent. Dent had held the chairmanship from 1880 following the death of George Leeman. Leeman had risen to the post of chairman from quite humble origins, and it has been reported that 20,000 people watched his cortège. Dent on the other hand had benefited from the good fortune of his father, an impoverished farmer, who had inherited a very large sum of money from a distant relative. It was through a condition of this inheritance that Dent came to have the unusual Dent Dent name, the condition being that they adopt the family name Dent. John Dent Dent had been born John Dent Tricket.

John Dent Dent was succeeded by Joseph Whitwell Pease, who as has already been mentioned, was forced to resign following bankruptcy. Over on the Great Northern a very similar picture of change was occurring. Lord Colville of Culross stepped down as chairman in 1895, being replaced by W.L. Jackson, later Lord Allerton. Patrick Stirling, the Great Northern's most celebrated locomotive superintendent, died in office, also in 1895. Oakley's superintendent of the line, Francis Pickersgill Cockshott, retired in 1895 as did G.P. Neele, the London & North Western's superintendent of the line, though Neele retired in the May before the races and Cockshott did not retire until after the race was run.

Across the border in Scotland the Caledonian players were led by the general manager, Sir James Thompson, and the flamboyant Irvine Kempt was

*Patrick Stirling, the chief
mechanical engineer to the Great
Northern Railway. (National
Railway Museum)*

superintendent of the line. Kempt is described as being a very snappy dresser, 'in the manner of a regency buck', and was also cited as being behind one of the fastest start-to-stop runs in the country in 1900 (between Forfar and Perth), which was timed to take 32 minutes to run the 32.5 miles.

> It was initiated some fifty years ago during the time that Irvine Kempt was Superintendent of the line, and the tradition of fast running north of Perth has been maintained all down the years.
>
> Nock, *Scottish Railways*, p. 44

Irvine Kempt, like many other senior railway officers, took his turn at the Clearing House Superintendents Conference as did his rival on the Great Northern, Francis P. Cockshott. Kempt was also a friend of the London & North Western's superintendent of the line, G.P. Neele, and at Neele's retirement dinner, given by the Superintendents Conference, both Kempt and Cockshott made speeches in his honour. Neele was succeeded by Robert, later Sir Robert, Turnbull. The degree to which the senior officers of all the railway companies were integrated, furnishing each other with testimonials to prospective employers and other forms of mutual aid, when added to the dynastic tendencies already alluded to only adds to the incestuous air of railway employment practices.

The North British Railway was, at the time of the races, under the chairmanship of Lord Tweeddale, while management was in the hands of Henry Conacher, who was credited with improving, all round, the North British's performance. During the 1890s the North British did begin to pay dividends, but these were so low it is difficult to refer to them as successful. However, the reputation Conacher earned was not founded on share dividends, but on improved performances in operating. Lord Tweeddale had been elected chairman in 1886 and just before the races commenced he presided over the opening of the West Highland line which was ceremonially opened by his wife Lady Tweeddale and came into operation in August 1894. It was Lady Tweeddale who was on hand during the opening of the Forth Bridge, on this occasion agreeing to ride over the bridge on the footplate, only if the then general manager John Walker would accompany her. In Hamilton Ellis's book, *The North British Railway*, this incident and the fact that his statue stands in front of Waverley station are the only references to Walker, whose career was marred by disastrous labour relations and near chaotic operational procedures. Like its southern partners, there had been changes too at the top of the North British management structure. John Walker, who was general manager in 1888, had a stroke on the steps of Waterloo station in 1891, only months after presiding over a very bitter strike by Scottish railwaymen. Henry Conacher, who replaced Walker, was general manager on the Cambrian Railway before being offered the North British post. Conacher's application was supported by his friend Sir Henry Oakley and testimonials as to his abilities were sent by Sir Edward Watkin, Henry Pollitt and Christopher Tennant. Conacher chose David Deuchars as his assistant and his support for Deuchars against a member of the board eventually led to Conacher leaving the North British in 1899. Conacher's departure was created by the machinations of a director called Wemyss who accused him of fraud. Conacher, though innocent, resigned and despite attempts to reconcile him he refused to have any further dealings with the North British in particular and Scottish railways in general, and he eventually returned to managing the Cambrian.

Deuchars was a capable and well-liked man, especially in Dundee where he was posted before being promoted, going to Edinburgh as Conacher's superintendent of the line. Before departing, Deuchars was given a civic reception in honour of his contribution to the improved services offered by the North British. The *Dundee Advertiser*, often a stern critic of the North British, credited the new team of Conacher and Deuchars with improving the service and inspiring a new morale and confidence among the staff. Given the circumstances of the strike which marred the final months of John Walker's term as general manager, morale and confidence were much in need of improvement, especially so when one considers the intransigence shown by Walker in his dealings with the strikers.

The changes in operational, technical and managerial executives undoubtedly had a role in the decision to embark upon a fresh round of speed-based competition for traffic to Scotland. There was also the issue of what to do about the Empire State Express. The Americans, in the autumn of 1892, had taken the Blue Riband for the fastest, daily, long-distance journey with their Empire State Express service between New York and Buffalo, an honour which had been held up to that point by the London & North Western for its efforts in the races to Edinburgh in 1888. It would seem unlikely that this was a major factor in the decision to race, but it is likely that it was aired in the boardroom debate. The likelihood becomes an almost certainty when it is recalled that at the same time as the races were run the America's Cup races were taking place off the American coast and the progress of these races was reported alongside that of those to Aberdeen.

The seven years between the Edinburgh contest and the races to Aberdeen saw other important changes taking place, beside those of management personnel and locomotive design. Other than the opening of the Forth Bridge itself, from an operational aspect the most important change was the introduction of clauses into the Railway Regulation Act of 1889 concerning the provision of continuous automatic brakes on passenger trains, a requirement which affected the London & North Western more than most.

There were two other parts of the Act which affected the running of trains, both of which related to signalling issues. One was the insistence on interlocking, a mechanical locking system whereby the movement of signals and points could only be completed if the signal gave the correct indication of the point setting and the signal could only be set if the points were correctly locked in position, a method first introduced by Saxby in the 1850s. The second item concerned the establishment of the absolute block system, which essentially can be summed up as being the space between one train and the one following it. A block being the space between one signal-box's starting, or advance starting signal and the next signal-box's outermost home signal, only one train at a time is allowed to enter this section of track. The new regulations incorporated the latest development in signalling technology, electronic interlocking, albeit that the system had been patented over a decade earlier and had been fitted throughout the London, Chatham & Dover Railway's network since 1878.

The electronic interlocking signalling system was developed by W.R. Sykes and its first patent dates from 1875. Sykes's system was essentially an electrically controlled lock on the starting signal. The easiest way to visualize this is to imagine two signal-boxes, A and B. The signalman in Box A, using Sykes's system, could not pull off his starting or advanced starting signal until it was released by the signal 'line clear' from Box B, and the Box B signalman could not give 'line clear' to Box A until the train had passed the Box B starting signal and it had been lowered to danger – a giant step forward in railway signalling safety.

All these measures were in reality very basic safety features and yet it was almost sixty years earlier that passenger traffic had begun. Railway accidents had been a common occurrence, commencing with the running down of the MP and railway supporter William Huskisson at the opening of the Liverpool & Manchester, that is if one takes the Liverpool & Manchester as being the first genuinely public transport facility.

The only apparent reason for the delay in implementing, network wide, such basic safety measures, was that the companies argued that they needed to be given time to implement them, or that their own patently inadequate devices were in fact more than sufficient. Though there is also the possibility that with such a weight of Members of Parliament and lords with railway interests, any attempts to force change could effectively be blocked or severely amended in the committee stages as bills went through their parliamentary processes.

There were Standing Committees on railways in many of the years between 1838 and the 1880s. These committees investigated all manner of railway business and took evidence from many of the leading figures in railway history. In some of the earliest committees James Watt and George Stephenson appeared to argue the case about high pressure steam engines, Watt being opposed to them. In the 1840s another such committee took evidence concerning the conditions which prevailed in the railway construction industry and of the Woodhead Tunnel works in particular,

> The report was formally received. It was not even debated. . . .
> Nothing was done. But then, what was to be expected of a House of Commons where one railway company alone was said to have eighty Members in its pocket? . . . The story of the very great past at Woodhead is that of the two old tunnels, and that is a story of heroic savagery, magnificent profits, and devout hypocrisy.
>
> Coleman, *The Railway Navvies*, pp. 150, 115

Coleman may have been commenting on the construction of the Manchester, Sheffield & Lincoln Railway's major tunnel through the Pennines, but the remarks are equally applicable to other railway projects and indeed to other industries. A further example of Victorian hypocrisy can be seen in the mining industry. Speaking on the subject of mining in South Staffordshire, an assistant commissioner of the Children's Employment Commission made the following remarks:

> . . . we might consider the whole population as engaged in a campaign [ie, military campaign]. In Lancashire and Cheshire . . . accidents were a 'daily occurrence in almost every mine where numbers are employed, and so common that a record of them is seldom kept'.
>
> Gregg, *Social and Economic History*, p. 143

A bill to outlaw some of the worst excesses in the mining industry was put before parliament in 1842, where it passed its first two readings without a division. However, when it passed to the Lords,

> But the House of Lords which contained most of the mine-owners, and particularly Lord Londonderry, one of the richest of them, heavily criticised and amended the Bill. Londonderry persuaded the Lords to strike out the clauses which gave inspectors the power of reporting on the state and condition of the mines. It was more than sufficient, their lordships deemed, that inspectors should report on the state and condition of people in the mines.
>
> Gregg, *Social and Economic History*, p. 144–5

After noting the comments of various reformers, MPs, lords, and the victims themselves, Gregg sums up:

> In each case – factories, workshops, and mines – reform was carried out only after a long and painful struggle against the resistance of interested parties and the indifference of the uninterested.
>
> Gregg, *Social and Economic History*, p. 145

The abuse of power and privilege in amending, suspending, delaying and generally impeding parliamentary proceedings covering railway finances, operations or safety was matched only by the blatant insider dealing in railway company shares. Writing of the period 1876 to 1890 under a pseudonym, 'A Member of the 'House', the following appeared in *The Jubilee of Railway News*:

> The best days of the market were when Paris used to speculate in English Rails. They used to deal 'in lines,' one well known banker, if he had a tip given, often buying a million stock.
>
> What has killed this speculation in Home Rails, especially in more speculative stocks, was the way the 'shops' used inside information in the most unscrupulous way. If they had confined themselves only to using inside information it would have been bad enough; but some of them would think nothing of passing a tip to buy while they were deluging the market with stock through roundabout ways.
>
> A Member of the 'House', *'The Stock Exchange Home Railway Market'*,
> *Jubilee of Railway News*, p. 129

Any notion that Victorian business life and practices were in some sense morally, spiritually or practically any improvement on those of today's business or mercantile classes should be put aside. It may be true that there were some 'enlightened' ideas like those of Sir George Findlay, quoted earlier, though the degree of Sir George's 'enlightenment' did not extend to collectivization, for Sir George was as utterly opposed to trade unions as any of his railway peers. Often Victorian philanthropy was little better than self-interest: a fit and contented workforce produced more.

There were undoubtedly some Victorian entrepreneurs who would qualify as being philanthropic in their actions, but for every Robert Owen, or Titus Salt (who built Saltaire, providing decent housing, a church, a hospital and a library for his employees), there can be found dozens if not scores of dozens whose only interest was profit, and if workers had to suffer to produce it – so be it!

Victorian values have, since the late 1980s, been extolled as worthy and decent values to embrace. However, even the briefest of glimpses into the conditions of employment, the physical ill-treatment of workers, the lack of rights, the dangers to life and limb caused by unguarded machinery, the primitiveness of the technology and the lack of appreciation of the dangers of certain categories of production, the use of asbestos (a danger not admitted until the late twentieth century), phosphorus and the infamous 'phossy jaw', suffered by those in the match industry, all illustrate all too clearly the indecency of many of the 'Victorian values'.

Disciplined and educated workforces, like those of the late Victorian era, were not born, but were the result of a plethora of processes commonly lumped together under the banner of the 'Industrial Revolution'. In late Victorian Britain the process of industrialization was entering its second century, the barn-like water-driven factories of Arkwright, Compton and others had given way to huge four- and five-storey edifices containing hundreds of machines driven by steam, with thousands rather than hundreds of operatives under one roof. The degree of human cooperation to achieve this system of manufacture, is not, as some would maintain, a perfectly natural form of human endeavour and behaviour; it was brought about, in the first few decades of the nineteenth century, only by varying degrees of force, intimidation, coercion and brutality.

> But since the machines needed little skilled attention the cheap labour of children could be used. So the mill-owners entered into contracts with the Poor Law authorities of the towns for supplies of pauper children between the ages of seven and twenty-one. The Poor Law officials were only too glad to get rid of their child paupers, whom they were bound by law to apprentice, and contracts were made for batches of fifty, eighty, or a hundred to be sent to the cotton mills. . . . Generally these pauper apprentices travelled long distances from London and the South, where the pauper population was largest, to the North. If a mill closed the unwanted children were simply tipped out on to the roads and left alone to make the best way they could. To the cotton master they were as much his property as the machines they tended. Kind treatment did not pay.
>
> Gregg, *Social and Economic History*, p. 54

Frequently the inculcation of discipline was carried out by the imposition of sanctions and these sanctions ranged from fines deducted from the alleged miscreant's wage packet, through ill-treatment in the workplace, to periods of imprisonment and hard labour on the treadmill. Deportation was not uncommon, generally being reserved for those members of the workforce who dared question the authority and control of the owners by the creation of trade unions. Having been organized into groups by the process of industrialization the workforce began forming organized groups themselves to counter the power of the employers.

> The concept of people being broken in to obedience to the unnatural rules and routines of the mill, as a young horse is broken in, has something to recommend it.
>
> Thompson, *The Rise of Respectable Society*, p. 205

Overall the antagonisms between employed and employer, after about 1850 and until well into the 1870s, were largely submerged by a moderate improvement in

*The station staff of a North Eastern Railway station, probably Durham, at the time of the races. Though the station staff did not enjoy the status and kudos of the enginemen, they were equally important to the running of the railway and these men were the passengers' main contact with the company. (National Railway Museum)*

working conditions and the recognition on the part of at least some employers that the harsh discipline of the early decades was no longer necessary. By this time many of the workforce had little more than folk memory of pre-industrial society, and accepted a more or less regulated existence, essentially because that was what they had been born into. The individual was becoming bounded by employment practices, and a growing amount of state intervention in the sphere of social legislation. The need for and acceptance of institutional reforms in education, health and increasing numbers of 'social' organizations both charitable and non-charitable to deal with the social problems of disease, unemployment, electoral reform, drink, prostitution and gambling, all played their part in smoothing the way to a more orderly and 'respectable' organization of social existence.

At the time of the accelerations to Edinburgh of 1888 and the races to Aberdeen of 1895, a modest degree of unionization had taken place in the railway industry in the shape of the Amalgamated Society of Railway Servants, which dated from 1871, and the breakaway Association of Locomotive Engineers and Firemen, an exclusive union for the 'aristocracy' of railway blue-collar workers, the footplatemen, formed in 1880. The choice of the word servants in the title hints at the workforce's appraisal of their standing with regard to their employers. The following quote shows the extent of the subservience; though the quote relates to activities on the Great Western Railway, attitudes and conditions elsewhere were little different and the race companies were no exceptions:

To The Honourable Board of Directors, Humbly Sheweth,
    That your Memorialist approach your Honourable Board to lay before you the desire of your Memorialists, and regret that they should be compelled to make this third appeal to you for the withdrawal of Circular 3478, issued by Mr. Dean, 1st October 1879, which increases the hours of labour, and in many cases reduces the wages of your Memorialists, and ask your Honourable Board for 10 hours per day booking on and off duty, also 150 miles for passenger and 120 miles for goods to constitute a day's work. That no man receive less than 6 days if able to perform his duty; and we consider classification as put in Circular 3478 a very unfair thing between master and man; and being undismayed by the opposition you gave our second appeal, we, as workmen in whose hands the lives and property of yours and the public are placed, are convinced that, in justice to our employers and ourselves, we are entitled to a more merciful consideration from your Honourable Board, and for further justification we may mention that the increased anxiety, excessive speed, and additional number and weights of the trains, additional signals, and night duty we have to perform, alone is sufficient to lay claim to the suggestions in this Memorial, and which is necessary to the safety of ourselves and the benefit of our employers, and we also ask your Honourable Board to receive a deputation of the men to state their grievances, and place your Memorialists in the position they now seek, to obtain direct from the Board, as your Memorialists are at all times agreeable to accept any reasonable terms issued direct from you, otherwise would feel extremely grieved to state that we cannot possibly accept Circular 3478.
    And in conclusion your Memorialists ask for scale of wages to remain as in 1847 Circular, and express their gratitude for all past favours.
    Hoping you will give this Memorial your favourable consideration, with a view that the harmony that has hitherto existed may be strengthened, and that we may ever endeavour to merit the same, is the desire of your Memorialists.
    We beg to remain your humble servants, Signed by the delegates on behalf of the men.

Murphy & Field, *ASLEF 1880–1980*, p. 10

Despite the humility of the terms used in the letter to Dean from the Great Western men, the attitude of the railway companies was one of intransigence, laced with a rich vein of hypocrisy:

    . . . the railway companies consistently refused to recognise trade unions, on the grounds that they interfered with the discipline and obedience of their workers and jeopardised safety.

Thompson, *The Rise of Respectable Society*, p. 242

In answer to a parliamentary question on the subject of unions in the railway industry, as has already been mentioned, Sir George Findlay replied:

. . . might as well have trade unions in Her Majesty's Army as to have it in Railway service.

Sir G. Findlay, BPP, vol. 33 (1893/4)

That the railway employers should raise the issue of safety as a means of defence against trade union activity is the height of hypocrisy, a travesty even, as one of the major concerns of the union was safety, particularly that of their members.

. . . with the exception of a very few railway companies that recognised the necessity and acted upon it, it may be truly stated that the principal railway companies throughout the Kingdom have resisted the efforts of the Board of Trade to cause them to do what is right, which the latter had no legal power to enforce.

Col. Yolland of the Railway Inspectorate,
from Nock, *Railway Engineers* p. 239

The depths of the hypocrisy indulged in by the chairmen, general managers and others can be gauged from the following figures. In the years from 1875 to 1899, 12,870 railway employees were killed and 68,575 injured. The numbers for the years 1874–6 were 3,982 killed and 16,762 injured, or almost 20 people a day killed or injured in railway service. These figures do not mention the numbers of passengers and non-railway personnel killed and injured on railway property or in railway accidents. The total at work on the railway in 1895 was a little over 465,000. The accident figures relating to railway employees over the 25 years between 1875 and 1899 represent almost 10 deaths per week and more than 50 injuries per week, an appalling record by any standards, and one which it is difficult to imagine being made worse by the unionization of employees.

By twentieth-century standards the early demands of the railwaymen, union recognition, a ten-hour day, overtime at time and a quarter, and Sundays at time and a half, seem neither especially radical nor particularly excessive, and particularly so when one considers that in 1896 they were estimated as earning on average 24*s* a week. However, despite a grudging acceptance of the concept of a unionized labour force by some companies, others, like the Scottish companies, refused to recognize the request for union representation, leading to unrest and riotous demonstrations in Scotland. From December 1890 until February 1891 the men of the North British and Caledonian Railways were on strike, as for a time were the men of the Glasgow & South Western. Numerous grievances were involved in bringing about the strike; conditions at Waverley station have been cited as one of the more important ones.

During the six weeks of strike there were some very serious incidents of public disorder. In Motherwell the strikes led to evictions for some of those living in company tenements and houses. Demonstrations to prevent the evictions led to the reading of the Riot Act and the hussars being called out to restore order. During the period of the strike the station and signal-box in Motherwell and other sites were attacked with stones, blacklegs were frequently set upon and assaulted, and those trains which did run were also subjected to being stoned and vandalized by the strikers. This strike was also the first officially supported, in Scotland, by the Amalgamated Society of Railway Servants and only the second strike throughout the whole of the United Kingdom to be given official backing by the ASRS.

John Walker, the general manager of the North British, was the epitome of inflexibility and refused to deal with Henry Tait, the secretary of the Associated Society of Railway Servants in Scotland, or negotiate with the men until they resumed work. At the height of the strike 9,000 men were out, miners were staging sympathy strikes and there were mass meetings in Edinburgh and Glasgow.

Five years after the unrest in Scotland, in 1896, Nock's 'commander-in-chief' of the London & North Western, Frederick Harrison, dismissed a great many men who had joined the Amalgamated Society of Railway Servants, but such was the public outrage that the men were re-engaged. The available evidence suggests that the railways were slow to accept unionization of their workforce and this was, if anything, against the trend of industrial practice in the late 1880s and early 1890s.

> What did happen in the 1890s was not so much the long-delayed emergence of a coherent and homogeneous factory proletariat, as a surge in collective activity, across a broad cross-section of the working classes and across the boundaries of skill and status. This was accompanied by a shift in the character of union activity from dominance by the concerns of individual workshops and plants, to control and leadership by union officials in pursuit of more general industry-wide strategies. It was a move welcomed and encouraged by most large employers, who, aside from the railway companies, saw the advantages of collective bargaining conducted with responsible union leaders for securing peaceable labour relations, uninterrupted work, and predictable production at settled labour costs.
>
> Thompson, *The Rise of Respectable Society*, p. 244

In London between 1886 and 1888 there had been demonstrations in support of demands for the nationalization of land, mines and railways. There was even an early attempt to create an organization similar to the Transport Users Consultative Committee; this was the ill-starred Railway Nationalisation League whose 1895 manifesto was reported thus, in the *Railway Times*:

There is something impressive, almost of a flesh creeping nature, in the sound of the word 'league'; but the pleasurable anticipation of horror with which we turned to the Railway Nationalisation League's Manifesto were scarcely fulfilled. For this document is composed partly of harmless statistical information of the Bradshaw's manual type, and partly of some flatulent stuff which looks like the fag end of a Socialist programme.

*Railway Times*, vol. LXVIII, no. 4, 27 July 1895, p. 461

In 1889 there was a major strike by dockers in London's West India Docks that received great public sympathy and support, and not only in Britain, for over £30,000 was raised in Australia and sent to help the strikers. Despite the problems created by a docks strike, public support was forthcoming because the employment conditions then prevailing on the docks were very poor, with low wages, badly rated piece-work and a pernicious system of casual labour,

Even when employed the earnings of the 'casuals' were so little that they were immediately consumed in food. One or two workless days meant nothing to eat, and returning to work on an empty stomach. A few hours work in this condition and the docker was compelled to 'pay himself off' in order to get a little cash to stay the pangs of hunger. Thus, even when work was available, he earned less than he might have done, and set up the whole vicious circle anew.

Gregg, *Social and Economic History*, p. 390

The demands of the striking dockers was for a pay rate of 6*d* an hour, a minimum engagement time of four hours and extra pay for overtime – even less of a demand than that put forward by the railwaymen in their first unionized negotiations with the management.

In broad terms the trade union movement doubled in size between the London dock strike and 1892 rising from 750,000 members to 1.5 million. The growth of trade union activity was paralleled by a rebirth of the socialist tendencies of earlier in the century and the intellectuals of the day were hotly debating the end of capitalism. The growing labour movements and the legislative changes in employment practices were only one area of difficulties with which railway management in the 1890s had to deal. In Victorian Britain the railway was the major component in the distribution system, the disruptions to traffic and revenue caused by events like the London dock strike or strikes by miners not only affected traffic movements, but could and did have significant impacts on profits and on dividends.

Strikes in the coal mining industry, in particular, affected the railways, not only because a great deal of railway business included the carriage of coals, but also because the railways themselves were major coal users. Strikes by miners in Scotland in 1894 seriously affected both the North British and the Caledonian, and the Scottish coalfields were by no means the most militant, nor were they the largest of the coal-producing areas. In Victorian times almost the whole of industry was steam driven, so mining strikes affected practically every area of manufacture, including gas making, spinning and weaving, iron and steel trades and, as the railways were carriers to all these industries too, the knock-on effects of mining strikes could and did stretch way beyond the confines of the pit.

A strike by miners in Durham over reductions in pay began on 12 March 1892 and lasted three months:

> All the Durham mines closed down, and most of the blast-furnaces throughout the area in consequence had to be damped down; many other works were affected; and Tyne Dock and other docks around the coast were practically at a standstill until the strike was settled 12 weeks later. During this time the N.E.R. passenger train services had to be greatly reduced and mineral traffic practically ceased.
>
> Allen, *The North Eastern Railway*, p. 227

The nature of railway organization and operation in late Victorian Britain on occasions created circumstances in which individual companies could benefit from unrest in other industries. Strikes by miners in the Yorkshire and Midlands coalfields led to extra coal traffic for the North Eastern Railway when the mines in Durham and Northumberland were utilized to make up the shortages caused by the strike, which lasted from the beginning of August until nearly the end of November 1893. This form of activity was not only a crude type of strikebreaking it was in part responsible, some years later, for motivating the trade unions in the railway, coal mining and steel industries to attempt cooperation as the means to prevent strikebreaking by the employers shifting the production to areas and producers not affected by strikes.

Railway management was affected by union activity, as the previous examples demonstrate, in ways beyond its own control, though there were some cross-company, cross-industry board memberships which would have had some influence, but insufficient to prevent or end any particular dispute. The Scottish brewer Younger was a member of the board of the North British, but there is no evidence that his presence influenced the outcome of the strike in 1890/1. Perhaps these experiences make the directors and chief executives of railway companies more than usually anti-union, or perhaps it was the military influences from the early years. Whatever the reasons for the recalcitrance at the time the races were held, the attitudes and postures of the railway company executives flew in the face of what was taking place in other areas of industry and social life.

Like the majority of his peers in the railway industry, the general manager of the Great Northern, Sir Henry Oakley, was implacably opposed to the unionization of the workforce, yet at the same time he is described by some commentators as being paternalistic, and for many years he played an active part, as chairman, in the affairs of the Railway Benevolent Institute. This attitude is not unlike that of Findlay with the London & North Western and it seemed to be something of trend in Victorian social attitudes among not only the ruling class but also in large sections of the managerial class. It is as if paternalism and 'good works' in some areas, such as orphanages, church or chapel, even helping the distressed daughters of gentlefolk, did, in some mystical and unexplained way, make up for draconian and reactionary methods in the spheres of work, social justice and individual liberty.

Men such as Oakley, or Harrison, his opposite number on the London & North Western, and their counterparts on the other railways had and did spend their entire working lives in a degree of comfort and security far beyond anything enjoyed by their employees. The average railway worker's earnings in the 1890s was less than £100 per annum. As early as 1870, Patrick Stirling, for instance, was paid £2,500 p.a. on taking the post of locomotive engineer to the Great Northern. At Crewe, where F.W. Webb was chief engineer, he was being paid £7,000 p.a. by 1890 and on his death in 1906 left almost a quarter of a million pounds, a huge sum for the time. The salaries of higher management in the same period were like that of Stirling and Webb, in the thousands per annum and then of course there were the dividends on shares and sundry other emoluments.

Stirling's obituarist in the *Railway News* described Stirling thus:

> Like most true Scotchmen, Mr. Stirling was an intense conservative at heart. It is questionable whether he ever entirely reconciled himself to the use of the Automatic Continuous brake, nor had he much sympathy for such new-fangled ideas as bogey carriages and third class lavatories.
>
> *Railway News*, November 1895, p. 704

Many a text on railway history is littered with references to the severity, taciturnity, remoteness, aloofness and 'natural conservatism' of the railway managers, locomotive engineers and other high-ranking officers. The overall effect of this gives the impression that they were a stern and foreboding crew whose only interests were the production of profit to pay the shareholders dividends. There is much to recommend this view, but the lives of senior railwaymen was not all work and church, some of them did find time for, and enjoy, a range of pastimes.

One locomotive engineer, to whom many of the adjectives used in the last paragraph have been applied, was the aforementioned Francis William Webb, chief locomotive engineer to the London & North Western Railway during the race era. However, there is evidence to suggest that Webb enjoyed music, cricket and gardening. He was a founder member of Crewe Cricket Club, and president of both Crewe Philharmonic Society and Cheshire Agricultural Society in 1887. Webb's interest in horticulture led him to seek ways of reducing smoke pollution in the works and it can even be argued that he had a sense of humour, as these comments from an interview given to the *Railway Magazine* in 1900 indicate.

> We make all sorts of things in Crewe Works – down to artificial legs and arms for poor fellows who lose their limbs by accident in the service of the LNWR.
>
> *Railway Magazine*, vol. 6 (1900), p. 104
> from Spink, *F.W. Webb*, p. 5

Webb controlled a very large workforce – more than 18,000 men and women were under his jurisdiction as chief mechanical engineer, of whom around 7,500 were employed directly in the works at Crewe, which at the time was the largest factory in the world. The relationship between Crewe and the works can perhaps best be illustrated by the following figures. In 1891 the population of Crewe was 28,761; with 7,500 in the workshops and with all those employed in the engine-sheds, station, signalling, porterage, etc., almost two-thirds of the town's working population were employed by the London & North Western in one capacity or another.

There is another aspect to the relationship between the Crewe Works and Crewe town, which does much to illuminate management thinking. There existed something of a history of political antagonism between town and works particularly over the political balance of the council and appointments to it by the railway company. Webb was 'made' an alderman and in 1887 mayor; his successor in the works, George Whale, was mayor before him. Though it is claimed that Webb was a reluctant politician, the same cannot be said for the company as a whole.

> His relations with the Crewe Liberals, who were largely Non-conformists, became strained as a result of the determination of the railway authorities to maintain their political grip on the newly incorporated town.
>
> Chaloner, 'Francis William Webb (1836–1906) of the London & North Western Railway', *Transport History*, p. 174

The philanthropic side of Webb's character was manifested in his championing of education, and technical education in particular, though this should be tempered with the knowledge that Crewe Mechanics Institute was supported by the company, who naturally had a vested interest in a steady supply of well-trained engineers, draughtsmen and fitters. Another incident, this time within the works, has less than philanthropic overtones – 150 workers were sacked in 1885 for being 'Liberals or Radicals'. While at least some of the blame for this can rightly be attributed to the company doctor, Webb cannot possibly have not known what was being done, as the doctor in question was also Webb's friend. Did the railway company really believe that because they began the settlement of Crewe they owned it? Was it an extension of the paternalism of the 'company knows best' philosophy into the social life of the town? Was it the greed for power and position of ambitious individuals within the management hierarchy? Whatever the answers may be, one thing is indisputable, neither the London & North Western Railway nor Crewe Works (a small part of which is now a heritage centre), are with us today, but Crewe undoubtedly is.

In the years between 1888 and 1895 there was a very important shift in the relationship between the railway companies and the State. The incident that caused this shift involved Sir Henry Oakley to a considerable degree. Oakley was nearing the end of his railway career when the races of 1895 were being run; he retired after twenty-eight years as general manager in 1898, though he did not give up his railway interests entirely, maintaining his post as honorary secretary of the Railway Companies Association until 1900. This post was far from honorary, and Oakley was regularly involved in many of the negotiations between the railway companies and the Board of Trade on matters such as railway safety, and rates and charges. In the period just prior to the races, there was a substantial rise in railway rates, a rise which Oakley himself cautioned against.

The decision to make the rises was, as Oakley feared, a grave error of judgement on the part of the railway companies. The repercussions which ensued from the new rates also lend weight to the argument that the Races to the North can be seen as a pinnacle of railway proficiency.

> He [Oakley] counselled in vain against the massive increase in railway rates which led to the unprecedented statutory freezing of these charges in 1894, and which signalled *the end of laissez-faire as far as British railway regulation was concerned* [my italics].

> *Dictionary of Business Biography*, vol. 4, M–R, p. 471

Throughout his long service with the Great Northern, Oakley was seen as being methodical, having an excellent grasp of administrative detail, and as an instigator of actions rather than a follower of trends. A keen promoter of the Great Northern, he was in the thick of things in a fares war with the old enemy at Euston early in the 1860s. In the 1870s the battleground was the South Yorkshire coalfields, the foes at this time being the Midland Railway. Another area of operations which Oakley had a hand in was the promotion of holiday traffic, such as that to Skegness, a growth industry in late Victorian Britain.

In 1888 and again in the 1895 races themselves, Oakley was very much the driving force on the East Coast side, ably assisted by his superintendent of the line, Francis P. Cockshott. Cockshott held this senior post for thirty years from 1865 to 1895. There is a hint in Nock's work on the races that Cockshott was not overly keen on the idea of high-speed running, yet in a brief biographical sketch in his pocket encyclopedia, Nock says of him:

> In his 30 years of office, made the G.N.R. the fastest line in the world. He held the belief that speed brought traffic . . . His greatest success was during the summer of 1888, during the first Race to the North, between the 10am departures for Edinburgh from Kings Cross and Euston, when he kept the East Coast service consistently faster than the rivals.

> Nock, *Railway Enthusiast's Encyclopedia*, p. 314

Whatever Cockshott's attitude there is the probability that the most important influence on the East Coast triad in the races of 1895 was neither Cockshott nor Oakley, but a quite remarkable telegram from the chairman of the North British, the Marquis of Tweeddale, to his general manager, Henry Conacher:

> My opinion is our best policy is to beat them at any cost and having done it proceed [to] remonstrate. Stalbridge [Lord Stalbridge, chairman of the

London & North Western] has always complained of the speed being too great and has suggested more moderate speed, but the present is [a] deliberate and well considered attempt to show what they can do, and we should strive to win.

Nock, Railway Race to the North, p. 79

The seeking of Tweeddale's opinion could be interpreted as part of a strategy by Oakley to secure the agreement of the other East Coast companies to become involved in yet more competition with the West Coast route, which had accelerated its 8 p.m. Euston–Aberdeen service to secure arrival in Aberdeen before the corresponding East Coast service. It was at Oakley's request that Conacher had contacted his chairman, and the whole purpose of the event seems to have been designed to do little other than provide Oakley with all the authorization he would need to take whatever action he deemed necessary in any response to the West Coast alterations to timings of the 8 p.m. Euston–Aberdeen.

The interesting feature of Tweeddale's telegram is its 'beat them at any cost'. No hint of mealy-mouthed 'accelerations' here, indeed the only possible interpretation is one of 'Go for it.' No doubt being a member of the aristocracy does give the individual a certain cache – one which is frequently notable by its absence among the members of the upper middle classes who formed the backbone of senior managerial positions in the railway and many other industries. All too often class membership, rather than ability or temperament, has been the major determinant in securing positions of responsibility and power within industry. Much of the current malaise of British manufacturing industry can be traced back to attitudes and practices directly attributable to class membership and the perceived value of such status, which countless other individuals strove in vain to emulate, if not directly, then certainly in matters of consumption of goods and services. Victorian Britain and especially the latter years of the period, can arguably be described as the point in time in which the upper middle classes were taking control of parliament, and consolidating its hold on economic power in the process.

Returning to his history of the Great Northern, O.S. Nock states,

While in the earlier contest, in 1888, it was unquestionably the East Coast that had forced the pace, in 1895 the initiative was with the West Coast from start to finish. At Kings Cross, York and Waverley [head offices, respectively, of the Great Northern, North Eastern, and North British Railways], it was a case of 'We don't want to race, but by Jingo if we do . . .'

and then in the following sentence,

Jackson [W.L. Jackson, chairman of the Great Northern] disliked it thoroughly, Cockshott constantly urged caution in running, but Sir Henry Oakley, like the great railwayman he was, determined to beat the West Coast at their own game, . . .

Nock, Great Northern Railway, p. 112

There seems to be a conflict between 'Cockshott constantly urged caution in running' in the above quote, and the remarks 'made the G.N.R. the fastest line in the world. He held the belief that speed brought traffic', quoted previously from *The Railway Enthusiast's Encyclopaedia*, also by O.S. Nock.

There is a similar conflict in the run-up to the Marquis of Tweeddale's sensational 'at any cost' telegram, which makes it possible to interpret Oakley's telegram asking Conacher to contact Tweeddale as being Oakley manoeuvring round a reluctant chairman, 'Jackson disliked it thoroughly'. In *The Railway Race to the North*, Nock says,

> And now Sir Henry Oakley hesitated before calling upon his allies for a further acceleration.
>
> Nock, *Railway Race to the North*, pp. 78, 106

This is prior to the sending of the telegram and following discussions with the chairman, Jackson. The telegram which Oakley sends to Conacher reads,

> My Chairman would like opinion of your Board as to desirability or otherwise of his communicating with Lord Stalbridge re acceleration of Scotch trains. Reply.
>
> Nock, *Railway Race to the North*, p. 79

*Lord Stalbridge, the chairman of the London & North Western Railway. (National Railway Museum)*

Nock's interpretation of this telegram is that it is unlikely that Frederick Harrison, the general manager at the London & North Western, would call off the accelerations. Therefore, in Nock's view, perhaps by an appeal to him from his chairman, he can be persuaded to call a halt. However, it is equally possible to interpret the telegram, as Tweeddale does, as being a request for clearance from the top to overcome the West Coast efforts. If Oakley was the 'great railwayman' Nock claims and he was 'determined to beat the West Coast at their own game', then what he would have needed was authority to race and when he did not get it directly from his own chairman he arrived at his goal by a different route.

From what has been recorded of Oakley's career with the Great Northern it is more than possible that he was looking forward to the contest, particularly if one recalls the challenges thrown out to the Midland over the services to Leeds or the battles for coal traffic in South Yorkshire, and that seeking Tweeddale's opinion was Oakley's way of circumventing his own newly elected chairman's reluctance to mount a serious challenge. The telegram to Conacher is vague, it smacks of fishing for opinion and just as Nock missed the point over Acworth, Scott and others being briefed by the management, he seems here to be misunderstanding Oakley's motivation. After all if Oakley wanted to beat the old rivals at their own game he could hardly do so if his own chairman thoroughly disliked the idea.

At the half-yearly meeting of the London & North Western Railway's shareholders held on 13 August 1895, barely a fortnight after Lord Tweeddale's telegram to Henry Conacher, it was reported that Lord Stalbridge

> asserted that there had not been such a thing as racing, but the North Western company had simply gone on in their way determined not to lose the traffic they had been in some danger of losing. The question as to who began it was not worthwhile discussing that day – it was a question between the company and the East Coast, and he thought it would be seen in the end that the North Western Company were perfectly justified in the course they had taken.
>
> *The Times*, Wednesday 14 August 1895

The point Stalbridge is making is a fair one if, as has generally been accepted, the West Coast accelerations were in part brought on by the East Coast's opening of the Forth Bridge. There can be little doubt that the opening of the bridge by the East Coast made travel over its route a more attractive proposition; it was a popular route before the bridge opened and that they gained traffic as a result is doubtless. The East Coast partners cannot possibly have imagined that the West Coast partners would not mount some form of response. In this scenario the West Coast's decision to accelerate is not only a justified response, in view of the Forth Bridge opening and its effect on the distances travelled, it is perhaps the best response, both as traffic winner and as an operational response to the changed operating positions now that the bridge was in service.

At the time of the races the managements of all five companies faced the same forms of pressure, and in 1888 the accelerated timings to Edinburgh did show some rewards in increased traffic – a factor which no doubt influenced Stalbridge's choice of words later on in his statement to the shareholders:

> He would not say that certain marches had been stolen on them [the accelerations of 1888, the admission of third class to the 10 a.m. ex-King's Cross and the more direct route afforded by the opening of the Forth Bridge], but certain advantages had been taken by others which in the opinion of their company ought not to have been taken, and they therefore determined to show, once and for all, that they were resolved to have their fair share of the traffic to the North. They might have heard that the cost of these excessive speeds and so on came out of the shareholders' pockets – that it was an amusement to the directors, but that the shareholders paid for it. That was not the case, because their return from the Scotch traffic hitherto showed that what they had done had been of great pecuniary advantage to the North Western Company. . . . in the end that the North Western Company would not be last in the race, whatever happened.
>
> *The Times*, Wednesday 14 August 1895

These incidents show the level at which the contest was being conducted, the company chairmen, general managers and their operating officers were all totally committed in the quest for trade. It might be argued that this episode demonstrates classic market forces: competition was reducing travelling costs and journey times, which was improving the products. However, as was shown at the close of chapter one, the railways were already experiencing fiscal difficulties and this was occurring despite growing levels of passengers carried and freight hauled. It is fair to say that Stalbridge did have a point as the Scottish traffic did increase after the races of 1888 and the London & North Western did benefit financially, as Stalbridge contended and the *Railway Times* concurred:

> . . . abundantly justified from a pecuniary point of view.
>
> *Railway Times*, vol. LXVIII, no. 8, August 1895, p. 250

The ending of an era is, in these middle years of the 1890s, quite unmistakeable considering the number of senior posts in most of the competing companies changing hands in this relatively short period of time, not to mention the impending *fin de siècle*. Changes were also occurring in areas way beyond the command of railway company directors, especially in social attitudes and particularly in relation to the way in which the working classes were beginning to organize politically and insist upon a more equitable distribution of wealth and power. Only weeks before the races began, this little gem appeared in the railway's trade paper, the *Railway Times*, under the headline 'Practical Anarchy'. The author quotes the written defence to the magistrates' court of a Mr Leggat of West Ham (a borough of London), who has had the temerity to travel upon the railway without buying a ticket – 'fare-dodging'! Another Victorian value?

I am an Anarchist, and refuse to recognise the right of a section of parasites, calling themselves shareholders, to make rules, regulations and bye-laws, own railways and monopolise the results of the united labours of thousands of working men, and then dictate upon what terms they should travel. I only recognise one class – viz. the working class who produce all the wealth of the world [see Marx, K., *Das Kapital*, on the surplus of labour] and are therefore the only useful class, and the only class entitled to ride.

The others – viz., politicians, law makers, judges, the modern Solomons called 'magistrates', retired soap boilers, gamblers on the Stock Exchange, exploiters, aldermen, sky-pilots, bishops, and the host of parasites who do not work but live in luxury and idleness, should be compelled to walk. . . . I shall demand comfort when possible for the class to which I belong, and that if that be a crime I shall be proud to be a criminal. He who would be free, himself must strike the blow. Long Live Anarchy, and to h–ll with Government!

*Railway Times*, vol. LXVIII, no. 1, 6 July 1895, p. 17

This sentiment was not without its sympathizers, both then and now. While this was not entirely the view of railway managements, there were some sympathies for classless travel, even among the railway managers. In August the *Railway Times* reported a meeting of the Cambrian Railway shareholders at which the chairman, Mr Buckley, presented a paper on the abolition of the three classes of travel, with the substitution of a small fee for privacy. The scheme which Mr Buckley advanced was also seen as a possible dodge for the non-payment of passenger tax. Those present at the meeting saw the remarks as a 'counsel of perfection' – that is, desirable but not practical. The *Railway Times* remarks that

it is significant that it should have been raised at a meeting of the railway shareholders, and the circumstance is an indication of the general trend of opinion in the matter of the class problem.

*Railway Times*, vol. LXVIII, no. 6, 10 August 1895, p. 177

In October's *Railway Times* there is a reply to the 'classless' travel lobby, which contains an important piece concerning the perceived attitudes of staff and management:

And as times grew harder, people, especially in the country districts, could no longer afford double prices for only one fifth better accommodation, and so the exodus from first and second classes to third-class gradually grew to its present proportions. Now, though the fares remain unchanged, the whole attitude of the companies towards their customers has undergone a revolution. The guards on the lines may still respect a first-class passenger, but the directors have little respect or regard for him. The third-class passenger has been placed on a pedestal, thanks to the enormous aggregate of receipts his journeys bring in.

*Railway Times*, vol. LXVIII, no. 14, 5 October 1895, p. 445

Railway company chairmen and their chief executives were not operating their railways in a social vacuum, but as leaders of major business enterprises they were frequently involved in the legislative affairs of state through their connections with both parliament and the Lords. They were also part of, and in some senses subservient to, the rest of industry in so far as they allowed the industry of the nation to be distributed, and they distributed to the nation's industry the supplies it needed to produce from. Chairmen and directors often held directorships or chairmanships in more than one company and in more than one industry, a factor which undoubtedly placed some forms of checking and balancing on the more extravagant behaviour of some railway managements. However, in the last decade of the nineteenth century railway chairmen, directors, and chief executives were all members of one of the most powerful industries in the country, with all that implies in terms of social standing, power and privilege.

Earlier in this chapter it was remarked upon that the railways did frequently operate in ways which the Board of Trade considered unsafe. The creation of vague and ambiguous legislation with only minor sanctions for non-compliance greatly assisted the companies in thumbing their collective noses at the recommendations of the Railway Inspectorate. However, not all the railway companies took 'a devil take the hindmost' attitude to safe operating practice, and following the 1889 Railway Regulation Act braking and signalling did improve enormously. The important factor here is basically one of confidence: the improved braking and signalling arrangements gave footplate crews greater confidence to run hard and fast, sustained over increasingly greater distances.

When they are not detailing the dates of opening, extension and amalgamation, or the construction of major pieces of civil engineering, in general railway histories tend to focus upon the performance of the locomotives and the terrain over which these performances took place. However, the real achievements of the races of both 1888 and 1895 are not those of the speed at which Beattock was ascended, or how fast a speed was accomplished, but the phenomenal degree of reliability exhibited by the two routes. For the locomotives to be able to deliver their part in the show, two routes, each of over 500 miles in length, owned by five different companies had each to operate as one coordinated whole. A broken signal wire, an unlit signal lamp, or delays to preceding trains, the possible permutations of things that could go wrong on a machine of this length and complexity are almost boundless.

There are any number of pitfalls involved in conducting an event of the size of the races, not least of which is that element usually labelled 'human error'. The miles of track, the countless signals and signal-boxes, stations, level-crossings, coaches, couplings, engine changes, coal, water – the different possibilities for errors are incalculable, and they are all subject to the inherent vagaries of human agency. To have an organization that is capable of maintaining a machine of such size and complexity is a considerable achievement in itself, to create an organization that can deliver near-faultless performances night after night for weeks at a time is surely a triumph for control. Hundreds of staff were involved in the races, and only if each of the individuals involved was correctly carrying out his instructions would the whole function at the required level of efficiency needed to create the circumstances under which the locomotive crew could deliver their part in the performance – fast and fearless running.

The demands placed on the organization and the technology available to support it were in some instances at the very limits of their capabilities, as will be seen when discussing the performance of the race crews in chapter three.

To run hard and fast an engine-driver must not only have confidence in his locomotive, he must also be confident that the track and signalling will deliver their part, that he will not leave the rails because of poor ballasting or alignment, that all the signals will be correctly set, after all it is upon these things as much as his own abilities that his and his train's safety depends. No amount of route knowledge or familiarity with the locomotive would save a driver from trouble in the event of a track or signal failure. Even if these were not fatal flaws, in any race situation they would be more than enough to cost victory. The races of 1895 tested the whole organization and at a much more fundamental level than the efficiency of particular types of locomotives. The whole chain of command, the effectiveness of the entire undertaking was subject to weeks of intensive pressure in maintaining the level of operational effectiveness needed to be able to race over a 500 mile course in the middle of the night.

The decision to race was, in the main, taken by men who had only recently been promoted to positions of authority, the major exceptions being Oakley and Cockshott, and to a lesser extent Lord Tweeddale, and Thompson and Kempt on the Caledonian. The choice of racing as a means to improve company fortunes has its roots in the use of speed as a sales ploy and as an important part of the advantages of rail travel, as indeed it still is. Though there were few external indications that the railway managers were aware of the threats to their supremacy, there were signs that serious difficulties were on the horizon. The decisions behind the races remain obscure, no doubt to save any embarrassment in the event of accident. Having made the decision to race, the London & North Western showed remarkable persistence in arriving at its winning time into Aberdeen.

Management in Victorian Britain had a far greater hold over the workforce than is usual in the latter decades of the twentieth century, though this rigidity did have a tendency to suppress useful innovation. It must also be said that it prevented the free flow of useful information feedback and thus deprived management of helpful material for successfully operating their companies. Viewing these problems in the context of railway development at the turn of the century only adds to the thesis that the races were the peak achievement in steam railway operation.

*Chapter Three*

# MEN, MOUNTAINS AND MACHINES

Running a railway is carried out at ground level by people who are usually lumped together under the banner of blue-collar workers. Some of them perform specialized tasks, such as engine-drivers or signalmen. There are also numerous semi-skilled grades, typified by the shunters and guards, together with huge numbers of unskilled workers – porters, carriage cleaners and permanent-way gangers – and in the Victorian era there were many other types of employment, which today have disappeared as a result of new technology or different methods of working. In relation to the racing of trains the most fundamental of the recent changes has been in signal technology. At the time of the races of 1895 the distance between one signal-box and the next would on average be a couple of miles, though of course there were stretches of track where signal-boxes were very much further apart, such as at Shap where there was little habitation with no junctions or crossovers, so the distances between signal-boxes could grow to five, six or more miles. Today one signal-box can control 100 miles of track and drivers can communicate with them via radio telephone.

The signalling staff have a very important role in the racing of trains – to them falls the task of ensuring that the racing train is not checked by their signals. This sounds easy enough in theory, but in practice it is complicated even when the racing trains are running to a fixed schedule; when they are running to no timetable other than the speed of the locomotive, then the signalman's task becomes somewhat more complicated. Keeping the track clear ahead of the racing train would involve the signalmen along the route clearing the tracks in ways not demanded of normal service conditions. Goods trains would need to be shunted into loop lines, stopping trains would be held in the platforms and services which would cross the path of the race trains at junctions would be held at signals until the racer had passed. The races would have been a fairly simple matter were it not for the countless complications caused to the official or, as it is known to the railwaymen, the working timetable, by operating one service in what can only be described as a rogue fashion.

Something of the difficulties involved can be gauged from the comments in a telegram from John Welburn, superintendent of the line on the North Eastern

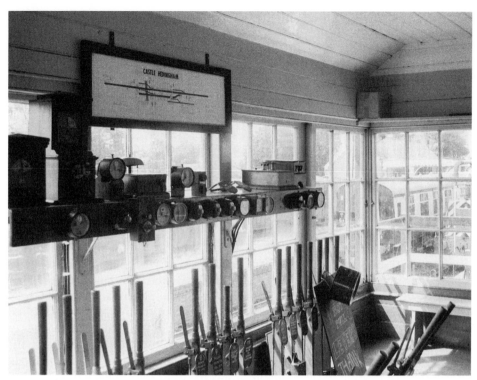

*Though this signal-box is at Castle Hedingham on what was one of England's lesser lines, the Colne Valley & Halstead Railway, its layout and instruments are not unlike those found in the signal-boxes of the competing companies in the 1890s. Each lever is numbered and has a brief description of what it's connected to, points, distant signal, etc.; the large panel labelled Castle Hedingham is known as the 'track diagram' and is marked with the same numbers as appear on the signal levers. The boxes and dials on the shelf below the track diagram are the block instruments through which the signalman can call the signal-boxes on either side of him. Others are position indicators which tell him whether the signals are set at clear or danger, or if he has a train on line in his section.*

Railway at the time of the races in 1895. After some preliminary comments on which stations passengers will be allowed to travel to on the race train, Welburn goes on to state, and in bold type:

> **Particular attention must be paid to the prompt telegraphing of the running of the express passenger trains referred to herein, and the margins hitherto observed between trains of lesser importance and the 8pm express train from Kings Cross must until further notice be increased to the extent of not less than ten minutes, and all concerned are to understand distinctly that the line must be kept absolutely clear for these trains to run.**

Nock, *Railway Races to the North*, p. 92

As the railway can be perceived as a machine, racing one train automatically incurs penalties in other areas of the system. The simplest example of this was the running of an extra service behind the racing trains to pick up and set down the parcels and passengers which the racing train did not stop or wait for. A more complex example would be the changes necessary at somewhere like Crewe, where the engines of the West Coast race train were changed. To ensure a swift change over of locomotives on the arrival of the racer, the signalmen would need to coordinate the movement of the incoming locomotive and train, and the movement of that locomotive from the train to another track. Then they would need to move the out-going locomotive from where it was being held and back it onto the train. Each of these movements would require the changing of signals and points in a particular sequence, it also required the signalmen to prevent any other movement which would conflict with those affecting the locomotive change-over. The effects of this latter condition could mean that other services were kept waiting until the race train had been despatched.

If the services which the race train kept waiting were connecting services, then delays occurred to those services that formed the connections; similarly if the waiting service was itself the connection then passengers were kept waiting. In this way the initial disturbance to the timetable spread throughout the entire service network. Keeping this disruption to the minimum was the responsibility of the superintendents of the line, but it was the job of operating staff to translate the plans from headquarters into the physical efforts of making them happen. Each of the contestants held meetings of their chiefs of staff at which discussions the decisions were made as to where savings in time could be made. Making these sorts of decision required a detailed knowledge of the route, the services utilizing it and the workers who operated it. These meetings would also have had to discuss ways to minimize disturbance and how to deal with both favourable comment and critical remarks.

The effective operation of the chain of command and the response of the links in that chain are of the utmost importance in operating a machine as vast and complicated as a railway. It is a long way in every possible sense of the word, from the boardrooms of Euston to the bleak isolation of a signal-box on Shap fells and, in a world for the most part lacking in telecommunication, it was inevitable that this type of communication had to happen. If the race was to be won communication had to happen quickly and accurately. The decisions to accelerate the services had to be communicated throughout the railway's operating departments and the only means was the telegraph.

> . . . but to hit the high spots and at the same time cope with all situations adverse to high speed over a 540 mile journey is a vastly different story . . .
>
> 'Scot', 'Our Story', *British Railways Staff Magazine*, p. 190

The 'vastly different story' referred to was high average speeds over short stretches.

The work of the signalman, vital to success in the races, was to an extent dependent on workers even lower in the order of things, such as lampmen whose job it was to ensure that the signal lamps were filled with oil, the wicks were trimmed, and they were lit after dark. Sir Henry Oakley may well have been a 'great railwayman' and might well have determined to 'beat the West Coast at their own game', but at the end of the day Oakley and all the other chiefs were dependent for success on the quality of the Indians in their pay – the lampmen, gangers, wheel tappers, shunters and myriad other grades who ran the railway at the grass roots level. For these men racing trains usually meant more work or a more complicated work pattern. There is some evidence that footplate crews on the race trains were given cash bonuses for their efforts, however, there does not appear to be any evidence that non-footplate staff involved in the operations of the racing trains were given any extra pay or inducement to secure victory.

When the races were being conducted almost a half a million people were employed by the railways. In the lower ranks porters, gatemen, crossing keepers and the like were frequently recruited either from injured navvies, who had helped in the construction of the line, or from local people, often former farm labourers. Moulding such an undisciplined and largely illiterate workforce into one which was capable of operating the railway system was a considerable achievement and, as has already been mentioned, it was a process which, as often as not, was achieved through a mixture of military discipline and draconian forms of punishment for even the smallest of errors, supplemented by an overarching paternalism among any number of managerial staff.

> For many years it was quite usual to commit railway servants to prison unjustly, and it must be a source of the greatest regret to every honest person to know that in very many instances the unfortunate men actually served long terms of imprisonment simply because jurors did not understand the practical working of railways; they appeared to consider that as some person had been killed by an accident that it was part of their duty to see that some railway servant was blamed or punished for manslaughter.
>
> Stretton, *Safe Railway Working*, p. 169

The men committed for trial following accidental deaths were hardly ever the managerial or boardroom gentlemen, it was the signalmen, drivers, shunters and guards who faced the wrath of the jury. Collisions, frequently attributable solely to the primitiveness of the brake technology employed, saw engine-drivers jailed and disgraced, even dismissed from the company's service and all because the equipment the company chose to use was inadequate to the safe operations of the train or the network. Though the men in question in the following quote were not jailed it was no thanks to the company;

> The resulting collision caused great loss of life. Driver Taylor and Fireman Davies were prosecuted for manslaughter. With ninety years of hindsight there is no question as to who were the guilty parties. Taylor had a clear road and the company admitted that the block signalling system, designed for operational safety, was out of action because of congested traffic. The directors of the Manchester Sheffield and Lincolnshire should have been in

the dock charged with gross negligence leading to manslaughter. But up to that time powerful railway companies represented by experienced lawyers had been able to load the blame on poor and inarticulate locomotivemen.

Not any more! ASLEF hired the best lawyers that money could buy and briefed them carefully. They tore the prosecution case to shreds and Taylor and Davies were triumphantly acquitted.

Murphy & Field, *ASLEF 1880–1980*, p. 19

This is the same incident which Colonel Yolland of the Railway Inspectorate cited as an example of the flagrant disregard of the Railway Inspectorate's recommendations. It is also an incident recorded in L.T.C. Rolt's book, *Red For Danger*, though the difference in treatment here could not be more marked; there is no reference to the suspended block workings, to Taylor and Davies's trial and acquittal, nor to the remarks of Colonel Yolland.

The driver of an express from Manchester to Hull overran signals and crashed into the rear of a race special which was standing at Hexthorpe ticket platform, killing twenty-five people. This accident was remarkable for the fact that the employees of the Company offered to forgo a day's wages in order to defray the cost of the disaster. It was an example of the esprit de corps and loyalty which pervaded all ranks of the old companies and which sounds, alas, like a fairy story today.

Rolt, *Red For Danger*, p. 85

Other forms of accident occurred where staff were found negligent, and in these cases it was not technology that was the root cause, but excessive hours on duty. In the present day working hours are, if anything, on the increase, despite the fact that fatigue could certainly be a major contributing factor in accidents, and that this is recognized as such is evidenced by legislation concerning the permitted hours of work of such people as airline pilots and long-distance lorry drivers.

In 1880s Britain signalmen were frequently required to work fifteen and a half or sixteen hours per day, six days a week – the negligence in these circumstances is much more likely to have been sheer exhaustion rather than any deliberate slackness on the part of the staff. Often the men involved had had many years of service with the company and were of a sober and conscientious nature. Stretton himself wrote on behalf of one man, the authorities conceding the point, but only halving the man's prison sentence; further action was required to have the man reinstated. Many did not have the backing of so distinguished an advocate as C.E. Stretton, civil engineer, and thus served their full prison terms, presumably finding other employment following their release.

There can be little doubt as to who were the real culprits – the men who owned and ran the railways. In chapter two the remarks of Colonel Yolland regarding the attitude of the companies to the introduction of Railway Inspectorate's recommendations were quoted. To them we can add Stretton's comments from a letter he sent to the Amalgamated Society of Railway Servants. Clement E. Stretton was a consulting engineer and his opinions were sought not only by the union but also by the government and his book, *Safe Railway Working*, was a standard text.

> It again furnishes evidence (if any were required) that the companies are not taking the necessary steps to arrive at the use of a general system [for train brakes], and it is very unsatisfactory to find that a considerable amount of rolling stock has during the past half year [1886] been fitted with inefficient non-automatic brakes which make no claim to fulfil conditions laid down by the Board of Trade, this practically placing that department of government at defiance.
>
> Stretton, *Safe Railway Working*, p. 97

In the circumstances there seems to be very little doubt that the directors and managers were equally, if not more, culpable than their employees. Not even the flouting of the recommendations of Her Majesty's Railway Inspectorate was sufficient to put them in the dock, nor keep their employees out of it. On occasion the sheer arrogance of the managerial staff is simply breathtaking:

> A driver on the North British, named Weston, complained to his fireman that he found great difficulty keeping his eyes open. I have been on duty 16 hours a day in succession and on the third day I went on the engine at 7.30 in the morning and left it at 11 or 12 at night. I took my meals on the engine. I never left the engine. I complained to my foreman and told him that I found great difficulty in keeping my eyes open. Upon the third day I told him that I could not hold myself responsible if anything occurred to the engine or the passengers and that it was unfair to force us to do it. He reported this to the Superintendent, Mr. Wheatley. He called me up and said 'Weston, unless you retract those words, I will dismiss you.' I said 'Mr. Wheatley, you have the power to dismiss me, but I cannot retract what I said.'
>
> Royal Commission on Railway Accidents, *1877*,
> from Murphy & Field, *ASLEF 1880–1980*, p. 15

What is indeed remarkable is that despite the privations, the long hours, and the arbitrary and draconian nature of railway discipline, people wanted to work for the railway companies. It is perhaps less remarkable when one considers the lack of provision for the unemployed – the workhouse was a far more hellish institution than the Great Northern Railway, or any of the other railways for that matter. However, the workhouse was an all too frequent repository for the families of railway men killed at work.

Greed and obstinacy cost the lives of hundreds of railway men and naturally the footplatemen suffered their share of casualties. Working conditions were appalling too – cabs open to every kind of weather, bucking and unstable

*The romantic view of life on the footplate: the gleaming paint and polished brass, even an oil can above the fire hole door – keeping the contents warm and thus easier to pour. This Great Northern crew typifies the late Victorian footplate crew and the high degree of cleanliness is the rule. (National Railway Museum)*

footplates and a permanent way where short cuts in material and methods of construction had often been taken.

If a railwayman was killed there was, of course no compensation for his widow and family. Unless they were very lucky, they were doomed to pauperdom and the workhouse.

Murphy & Field, *ASLEF 1880–1980*, pp. 8–9

Whatever the method of recruitment or the conditions of service, for many working people during the Victorian era there can be no questioning the desirability of a job on the railway. The railway was an expanding industry, for many reasons one at the forefront of technological development. It offered great opportunity for advancement on the one hand and secure and continuous employment on the other. Without a doubt there were men of humble origins who did find fame and fortune through employment on the railways, strange though this may seem to today's reader and with current perceptions as to the worth and social standing of those employed in the railway industry.

The 1890s in particular were a decade in which there was a great deal of uncertainty in various sections of the working populace, particularly among the most skilled members of the class. The steady rise in the size of the population and the growth of the mass market for certain types of consumer products during this period was leading to numerous tensions within the working class, particularly between the skilled and semi-skilled sections of the workforce. Examples from the railway industry would be the relationship and pay differentials between engine-driver and guard among the operating staff, or between a riveter and a machine shop fitter in the workshops. The railway was less affected by these new forms of tension than the shipbuilding and engineering industries; however, these types of dispute undoubtedly affected the relationships between the employed and their employers and the interrelations between different sections of the workforce.

There is no question that a great many rivalries existed between the employees of different railway companies even as late as the 1960s when my own railway career began, and when the lore of those distant quarrels still echoed. In the 1890s their strength was sufficient to generate partisan feeling from the House of Lords all the way up to the saloon bar. The feelings of partisanship extended beyond the railway employees to those men who rode in the race trains recording their speeds and regaling the public with tales of the events. However, it is worth recalling that these men were worlds apart from the men who worked the trains upon which they rode. Acworth became a Knight of the Realm, writing numerous articles, books and giving lectures on all manner of railway matters, particularly railway economics.

Acworth published articles and advertised his lectures in *The Engineer*, some of which were held in the John Street Adelphi for which there was an admittance fee of 5s, about what some engine-drivers were paid per day. There were a whole series of lectures on railway economics given at the London School of Economics; *The Engineer* commented:

> Mr. Acworth is well known as an unorthodox authority on railway economics. He holds certain views which are not regarded favourably by railway managers. But he is aggressive and he has much to say that is too really sound to be ignored . . . we gather that Mr Acworth would include railway economics in the domain of technical education. He wants railway economics to be made the subject of definite scientific teaching in this country.
>
> *The Engineer*, week ending 8 Nov 1895, p. 460

Charles Rous-Marten was another regular article writer in the pages of *The Engineer*, and he provided the magazine's coverage of the races, sometimes by travelling himself and sometimes relying on other correspondents to send him the details. Rous-Marten was probably the most widely known of the race correspondents, a magazine and newspaper editor whose articles appeared both at home and abroad. It was, though, his survey of Britain's railways on behalf of the governors of New Zealand that gave him his international reputation. The survey was most comprehensive, by all accounts, and Rous-Marten was commissioned to undertake others.

W.J. Scott was a man of the cloth who, in addition to tending his flock, wrote books and pamphlets popularizing the railways, the Great Northern being something of a favourite among them. Scott published several pamphlets, one of which was *Great Northern Speeds or the Fastest Running in the World*, another was *Kinnaber*, an account of the races, which sold for 1*s* per copy. This must have been a lucrative little sideline for Scott, as on occasion the demand for the pamphlets led to them being reprinted.

Another of the interested parties was a Scottish advocate, Norman D. Macdonald. All these men, in addition to riding on the race trains, were involved in a scheme put forward by the civil engineer, author and lecturer, C.E. Stretton, to create a railway museum at South Kensington. These men were as welcome in the management offices and boardrooms as on the footplate; for the most part they were given very privileged access both to compartments on the trains and to the company officers responsible for the conduct of the races. For this coterie of railway *aficionados* the races were a source of great entertainment, not to mention a possible source of income, and they spread that interest and entertainment far and wide with their tales of the night's events. Rous-Marten was for a time the editor of the *New Zealand Times* and it was his journalistic training and temperament which set the pace and tone of reportage:

> But the East and West routes are fighting out the matter to the bitter end, and with a grim and silent determination that seems to bode a tough and prolonged struggle.
>
> Rous-Marten, *The Engineer*, 9 August 1895, p. 125

*The Engineer* did not just give space to Rous-Marten's articles, a whole body of correspondence was published in letters to the editor. There were letters signed 'Big End', 'Traveller' and 'Passenger', one from Stretton congratulating Rous-Marten on his articles and others signed in the conventional style from Messrs Dowie and Forbes. The articles had also prompted a W.J. Baker of Hyde Park, Leeds, to send in a photograph of one of Worsdell's 'Rail Crushers' at work on the 'Flying Scotsman'. Photographs of moving objects were at the forefront of photography in 1895, and some of the world's first motion pictures were either of trains or of what was seen by the camera when it was mounted on the front of the engine.

The daily press took up the story and not only gave space to the races in the letters columns, they sent out their own staff reporters to cover the events, the *Manchester Guardian* even editorialized on the subject.

The value put upon the reportage by the railway companies can be assessed by the fact that the some of the companies involved appear to have provided a sleeping-car for the use of the literati, free of charge from King's Cross to Kinnaber Junction, from which point they had to pay full fare as they were then travelling on the Caledonian, that is, the West Coast's metals.

*A pair of Worsdells with a heavy East Coast train passes a permanent-way gang as it takes its load away from York. The difference between the cabs of these engines and the austere almost spartan ones of the Stirling and Holmes designs gives the Worsdell engines a much heavier appearance, and this may have contributed to the nickname of 'Rail Crushers'. (National Railway Museum)*

Though the telling of the story of the races would have been possible without the work of Rous-Marten, Scott, Acworth and the rest, it would not have been possible in anything like the same degree of detail, which extends to the knowledge that an unlit tail-lamp caused a delay to one of the East Coast race trains. The impressive point about this is that the unlit tail-lamp had been spotted, reported and acted upon in complete accordance with the company's rule book. Despite the explicit urgings of the management to cause no delays to the race trains, railway safety standards proved a more important motivator for the signalman, who wired ahead to stop the train and ascertain the reason for the lack of a tail-light, which in turn meant that the train failed to clear the section before the racer, a fact which meant that the racer was also brought to a stand, while the preceding train had its tail-lamp relit and drew clear of the running line. Nock illustrates the event:

Rous-Marten seemed to become thoroughly partisan for once and wrote in *The Engineer*:
    'But then 20 minutes had been absolutely wasted in delays at Dalton, Edinburgh and Dundee, in the first case by a blundering signal stop, and in the others by mere idling in the stations long after all was in readiness for the

start. These blunders were doubtless due to a misunderstanding, but they were grave blunders nevertheless, and resulted in making a present of an easy victory to the rival route.'

One could hardly call an extinguished tail lamp a blunder; it is just one of those things that must be taken amid the luck of the game; and even so Rous-Marten was exaggerating when he claimed that the time lost from these three causes amounted to 20 minutes.

Nock, *Railway Races to the North*, p. 103

The suspicion of partisanship is also evident in some of the writing of the Revd W.J. Scott.

. . . we ended by making it a panegyric of the G.N. solely because we found that line, measured by whatever test we took, to be well ahead of its fellows in the matter of speed, both in what it professed [*sic*] on paper and still more in what it really did on the rail.

Scott, *Great Northern Speeds*, p. 5

Over the border in Scotland, Norman D. Macdonald had access to both the Caledonian and North British officials. During the races of 1888 Macdonald was running to and fro between Waverley and Princes Street checking the arrivals of the competitors and during the races of 1895 he was riding the trains along with Scott and Rous-Marten. Macdonald, accompanied by W.M. Gilbert of *The Scotsman*, travelled to London especially to ride back on the race train, such was the level of interest and devotion to matters railway that possessed these men.

For the working railwayman involved in the races, life was very different. Railway growth, both in size and in the complexities of operation at the time of the races, had led to the existence of a large body of working rules and arrangements which were incorporated into various publications. These publications ranged through the *General Rule Book*, *Working Notices and Arrangements* and *Daily Notices*, which covered items such as permanent-way repairs and the speed restrictions in force on them. Then there were the working timetables and appendices to them, which covered the operation of the line and the features upon it such as sidings, loops, crossovers etc. Many of the salient portions of these publications had to be committed to memory by the engine-driver, who would have to know, in addition to all those items of the *General Rule Book* which applied to the working of trains, all that information from the *Daily Notices* which pertained to the route he would take, and likewise from the working timetable. He also had to have a high degree of knowledge about the steam locomotive and how to cope in the event of failures or breakages of the locomotive's components.

There is evidence that in some circumstances, particularly during strikes, certain companies were prepared to waive a knowledge of the safety rules and route knowledge, usually referred to by footplatemen as 'road knowledge', accepting that any new recruits had only scant knowledge of the locomotive. As long as someone worked the service, rules and road knowledge were conveniently forgotten.

> Unfortunately for the strikers, in the prevailing depression the authorities [management of the North Eastern Railway] found little difficulty in engaging men who were familiar [how familiar is a moot point] with the working of locomotives, and by arranging for members of the staff [scabs] to accompany these recruits [blacklegs] until they had become familiar with the lines, the signals and the rules, it was possible to introduce a provisional timetable with a fair service of trains.
>
> Allen, *The North Eastern Railway*, p. 139

Railway employment, in Victoria's reign, could be placed in the top ten industries in terms of pay and benefits, for many different grades of railwaymen enjoyed conditions envied by other sections of the workforce in general. Often the railway company provided some form of uniform, and great outings to the major seaside resorts were put on to entertain the huge mass of employees in the workshops. There were many company houses, even convalescent homes, in addition to those developing new towns like Crewe, Swindon or Wolverton which were almost entirely railway owned. However, by today's standards, working life was harsh, strict hierarchies existed, frequently based on length of service rather than ability, demanding varying degrees of obedience to more or less regimented codes of dress, behaviour and working practices.

In the footplate grades the link system established the pecking order, with crews progressing from the most lowly of turns – shed or station pilot, shunting the local goods yard or working branch line freight trains. Progress from the lower to higher links was generally by seniority, ensuring that the most experienced men were responsible for working the most demanding or premier duties at the depot. A similar system applied to guards and in a slightly amended form to signalmen as well, the larger and more important signal-boxes being manned by the more senior men, subject to the passing of examinations, thus making their posts dependent to an extent on ability in addition to seniority.

Footplate crew began their railway service as engine cleaners, progressing to passed cleaner, that is one who has passed the requisite test to allow him to work a train. In broad terms this was an oral test usually given by the shedmaster, and the cleaner being passed out had to know how to protect the train in the event of accident and a simple set of rules as to how to act if the train was detained by signals. In addition to some basic safety rules, the cleaner would need to know the essentials of how to build and maintain a fire, sufficient for the tasks the locomotive was to perform, how to operate the injectors and what sort of equipment the engine should carry when leaving the depot to enter traffic.

> In October 1885 I started work as an engine cleaner, the first step to being made an engine driver. . . . I took great pains to get the *Premier* the first on the line, as the premier is highest in the land. This engine worked a day train,

but only four times per week, as the men were booked to work 15 hours at a time; this constituted a 60 hour week, which was the rule at that time.

Talbot, *The London North Western Recalled*, p. 30

These bare details conceal a world full of customs and traditions, serious moments and prankish interludes:

There was a big staff of cleaners, one to every engine, marked to follow the working of the same whether night or day turn; and the cleaner had to clean the engine while the driver and fireman took rest. But, in this case [the author had been assigned to clean a goods engine used on a regular basis for a Manchester–Carlisle turn], it was what was called a double trip, which meant lodging at Carlisle for the driver and fireman; then the cleaner had to work every other day, doing something else to get his 54 hours of work in for the week. Amongst the cleaning staff there used to be many pranks played on one another, especially on a beginner.

Talbot, *The London North Western Recalled*, p. 30

The move from passed cleaner to full fireman was dependent on a link vacancy occurring in the lowest link. This would happen as the old hand passed fireman

*The cleaning gang at work on 0–6–2T No. 1054, which was designed for the London & North Western Railway by Francis William Webb in 1882. These locomotives became popularly known as 'Coal Tanks'. The locomotive is owned by the National Trust and is kept in service on the Keighley & Worth Valley Railway where it is a regular performer on their vintage train services.*

was made driver, each old hand fireman in each link would move up one link, thus creating the gap at the bottom, which would also be the link into which the newly promoted driver was placed. Passed fireman was the equivalent post to that of passed cleaner, the difference being that the passed cleaner was entitled to act as fireman and the passed fireman was entitled to act as a driver. That is, the passed fireman has successfully passed the examinations to become a driver, but does not have a vacant link position to move into.

Passed cleaners and passed firemen would only act in the higher grade when no other crews could be found to cover the duty. This meant that often these men had the roughest and most unpopular workings. Often these duties would be specials, or engineers trains, or other services outside the normal turns of the depot. When not acting in the higher grades the passed men would be confined to their normal duties, and to their lower grade pay rates.

When the crew of the racing trains began their railway careers items such as the continuous automatic brake and electronic interlocking were still to come and something of the conditions they faced can be appreciated from this incident:

> Towards the latter end of my time [as a fireman], my driver got removed, and I had to teach his successor the working of the engine and the signals; as he had never worked a passenger train before, he had never had to use a continuous brake, which, at that time was what was called simple vacuum. The action was the opposite to the automatic, that was to blow up to put the brake on. I had to work everything for two or three weeks.
>
> Talbot, *The London North Western Recalled*, p. 31

In a later chapter of *The London North Western Recalled*, driver Jameson talks about the conditions of the lodgings which the footplatemen stayed in when working 'lodging turns', which were very common, even in my own railway days in the 1960s. In his recollections, driver Jameson is referring to the work he was given to do before becoming a fireman, that is during his days as an engine cleaner.

> My next job was that of 'barracks lad'. The 'barracks' was the name given to the lodging houses provided by the company to house drivers, firemen and guards on double trip workings and specials. In the case of Patricroft [driver Jameson's home depot in a suburb of Manchester], it was a nearly new, solid Victorian building of three storeys and could easily have housed over 100 men. We did everything: washed the pots, and cooking gear, scrubbed the bedroom floors (cubicles these were and held a single bed and chair), made the beds and changed the bedclothes, and even did the washing with the help of a cleaner every Monday.
>
> Talbot, *The London North Western Recalled*, p. 36

Though the quotations have been taken from the accounts of a Manchester-based footplateman employed by the London & North Western, the men who crewed the race trains had all been through some system broadly comparable with the one outlined above (local and company variations notwithstanding), and were subject to approximately similar conditions of employment and very similar working patterns. However, despite the link system, the crews of the race trains were limited in number and there does seem to be more than a suggestion that some of them were hand-picked for the job. Crew choice was also to an extent engine choice, because at the time of the races it was the practice for a locomotive to be shared between two crews, rather than the system of common usage which came into practice later in the twentieth century.

During the race period, 15 July to 22 August 1895, the Crewe–Carlisle section was worked by only six different locomotives, with five drivers and firemen. One of the crews, driver Parry and fireman Nicklin, only made the journey once. Of the locomotives, the vast majority of the runs were made by engine No. 790 *Hardwicke*, which made nineteen of them, next was engine No. 1213 *The Queen*, with eight trips. The runs made by *Hardwicke* were shared between drivers Howman and Robinson and their firemen were Harrison and Wolstencroft

*After* Hardwicke *another of the race stars was No. 749* Mercury, *which put in twelve turns on the Euston–Crewe leg of the West Coast route, including the first accelerated running of 15 July. No. 749, with a train 16 tons heavier, equalled No. 790* Hardwicke's *average of 56.4 m.p.h. over this part of the route, which was the highest average set by the 'Precedents' over this section during the racing. Here, No. 749* Mercury *awaits the 'off' as the driver watches the photographer. (National Railway Museum)*

respectively. The workings handled by *The Queen* were by drivers Phillips and Rowe with their firemen being Kay and Hughes respectively.

A similar pattern can be seen in the locomotive workings on the Euston–Crewe section, and even here, despite her nineteen runs on the Crewe–Carlisle road, *Hardwicke* puts in an appearance, being the service locomotive on the 4th, 11th and 18th of August. Engine No. 749 *Mercury* covered twelve runs, No. 394 *Eamont* also worked twelve turns and the remaining seven turns were covered by three locomotives – No. 1309 *Adriatic* took four, and No. 1307 *Coptic*, No. 1683 *Sisyphus* and No. 1301 *Teutonic* took one apiece. Engine No. 749 *Mercury* was worked by driver Holt and fireman Hewins, while on No. 394 *Eamont*, driver Daynes was in charge with firing being done by J. Stinson. No. 1683 *Sisyphus*, like No. 790 *Hardwicke*, saw service on the Crewe–Carlisle road and was the first locomotive to record a 'mile-a-minute' time between Crewe and Carlisle during the races.

In Victorian Britain the railwayman enjoyed a favourable comparison with the working population as a whole with footplate crews enjoying a measure of affluence and social standing considerably in excess of that accorded to them today where their status, like the railways themselves, has declined with the growth of new communications and transport technology. As has already been mentioned, the footplate crews of 1895 were considered to be the aristocracy of the railway blue-collar workers whereas conditions for some of the lesser grades were considerably less pleasant than those that the engine-driver enjoyed. However, even the footplate crews were subject to a working week of sixty hours minimum, with a working day of ten hours and more, a six-day working week and only scant entitlement to holidays.

The engine-driver, because of the way in which the body of working rules and regulations had come into existence, had a good deal of authority and not a little prestige. In today's social climate the engine-driver is a relatively insignificant figure in the hierarchy of railway command structures and would be unlikely to be anything like the character of driver Clow of Rugby, whom Nock describes as:

> Peter the Dandy! Not for him the peaked cap and blue overalls of the traditional engineman; he wore a black tailed coat, tall hat, and an immaculately white shirt. In his spare time he kept a public house in Rugby, and ran a highly profitable business as a bookmaker.
>
> Nock, *Railway Races to the North*, p.97

The wearing of white shirts to work on the footplate may seem a little odd, considering the nature of the work to be performed, but seventy years on from the races, in my own footplate days there were still those drivers who did come to work in white shirts and it was said to me on more than one occasion, 'I come to work in a white shirt, it's your job to see I go home in one.' As to Clow himself he was driver on No. 1307 *Coptic* and also drove No. 1309 *Adriatic* during the race period, and with No. 1309 *Adriatic* made the Euston–Crewe journey of 158.1 miles in 157 minutes – a start-to-stop average of 60.4 m.p.h. Clow shared No. 1309 *Adriatic* with driver Walker and his fireman W. Hammond, and it was the Walker/Hammond team that was working No. 1309 *Adriatic* on the final night's racing.

On the Caledonian the crews whose names have remained on record are those of drivers Archibald 'Baldie' Crooks, Alex Brown, John Soutar, Tom Robinson and William Kerr. Firing for these men were Robert Smith with 'Baldie' Crooks, John Russell with Alex Brown, and David Fenton who shovelled for John Soutar; as to who fired for Kerr and Robinson, I cannot say. There are no records of which crews worked the race trains on the North British, though there are indications that on some occasions an Inspector W. McLellan was on the footplate of the North British race engine. The only name mentioned in connection with the crews on the Great Northern that my researches have located, is that of driver Falkinder. On the North Eastern there was a driver Miles Handy, who drove the Worsdell 'M1' class engine No. 1624 on the York–Newcastle leg on the night of 20/21 August. At Newcastle, driver G. Turner took over the train with 'M1' class No. 1621, and the only other name is driver Bob Nicholson, another of the North Eastern drivers. The only fireman's name to be handed down on the East Coast route is that of Tom Blades, fireman to Nicholson, who went on to become a star driver himself later in his railway service.

The descriptions of men who worked the racing trains range from taciturnity on the part of the Great Northern's driver Falkinder to 'fearless stop at nothing' as a characterization of the Crewe driver, Ben Robinson. The Caledonian pair of Archibald Crooks and Tom Robinson were next-door neighbours, living in railway cottages in a suburb of Carlisle. Despite being neighbours Crooks and Robinson are portrayed as being almost opposites.

> Both were first class enginemen, but while 'Baldie' Crooks was reserved and cautious, Tom Robinson was a veritable aristocrat of the footplate. Crooks, careful and economical runner that he was, hardly rose to a supreme occasion, whereas Robinson revelled in it. Always ready to share the thrills and fascination of his craft with those who were interested, Robinson became well known to the railway enthusiasts of the day.
>
> Nock, *Railway Races to the North*, p. 76

Another of the Caledonian drivers, John Soutar, is described as being an immaculately dressed gentleman with a white beard, who was so proud of his locomotive that he would give the engine cleaners a tip to keep the buffers shiny. Soutar also appeared, along with his locomotive, in a series of postcards printed and issued by the Caledonian by way of commemoration, and of course publicity. Driver Nicholson of the North Eastern gained a reputation as being a very hard and fast runner and certainly his average of 66 m.p.h. for the Newcastle to Edinburgh section of the race was a very fine effort, which was brought to the attention of the Press Association:

> The Press Association says it may be mentioned in connexion with the race to Scotland that the East Coast express yesterday morning covered the distance between Newcastle and Edinburgh – 124.5 miles – in 112 min. This

*The Caledonian 4–4–0s have Drummond pedigrees and, like their counterparts on the North British, modifications to the originals were made by subsequent chief mechanical engineers, No. 17 being Lambie's version. Driver Soutar poses with his engine for a picture for the Caledonian's publicity machine. Driver Soutar and No. 17 made some of the fastest running of the whole race, between Perth and Aberdeen on the night of 22/23 August when the West Coast set the record. (National Railway Museum)*

is equivalent to an average speed of 66.7 miles per hour, which constitutes a record rate of speed.

Press Association, from *The Times*, 22 August 1895

The Press Association did get the speed correct, and it was a record for the Newcastle–Edinburgh route, but there were higher averages set during the races and not least by the diminutive *Hardwicke* on the very same night when she ran the 141.1 miles from Crewe to Carlisle, over Shap fells, in 126 minutes – an average of 67.2 m.p.h.

Stirring deeds and records notwithstanding, it should always be remembered that footplate work is a team effort and one which is largely dependent, for its successful outcome, on a great many other people also doing their jobs to the best of their abilities. High speed running in particular is very demanding on the permanent way and therefore on the gangers who maintain it and the system of organization which makes the maintenence schedule regular and routine. In the case of the races, the maintenance was spread across five companies and over 1,000 miles of track.

That the races were run to such an exacting schedule, and one which was frequently beaten rather than simply maintained, for a period of weeks rather than days, makes the track maintenance a triumph of organizational control, though of course this sort of effort makes for a great deal less dramatic story than flying over the land at more than a mile a minute.

> At Cupar, Fife, it is said that the permanent way gang were called out nightly to correct the curve after the 'flyer' had passed; the average amount of distortion was about 3 inches. In passing these stories, which have come to me from persons who were living at the time of the race, I do not necessarily expect them to be taken for gospel.
>
> Nock, *Railway Race to the North* p. 83

Whether one takes the stories passed to Nock as being the gospel truth is not the issue; the wear and tear on the track would have been noticeable, though whether it was 3 inches nightly is perhaps less certain.

There is a tendency, among those who write about the railways, to talk in almost heroic terms about the exploits of the drivers, seldom giving credit to the

*Footplate work is in reality less about racing through the night and more about demanding physical effort, often in hot and cramped conditions. The fireman is cleaning clinker from the fire with a long metal shovel, frequently referred to as a 'paddle'. The fire is shovelled from the firebox and thrown off the footplate onto the ground. This would have to be carried out at the end of each turn of duty for the engine; if the turn was a long one it may even have to be done during the working shift as well.*

efforts and abilities of the fireman and failing altogether to mention the efforts of those not actually on the footplate. Undoubtedly the driver is in charge and responsible for all that goes on on the footplate, but it is the physical exertions and skills of the fireman that make it possible for the driver to make his locomotive perform to its utmost: 'No steam, no show.'

Having been a fireman myself, on numerous performances which have made it into print, I feel well qualified to speak on such matters. I was fireman to driver King of Nine Elms when he was driver on an enthusiast special, non-stop for the 122 miles from Waterloo to Yeovil, in the early 1960s. This run was, I believe, something of a record on the Southern Region of British Railways, which does not have water troughs. The importance and use of water troughs will be more comprehensively explained in chapter five, when dealing with the locomotive performances. All that needs to be said here is that this was the first time Waterloo–Yeovil had been run without a stop at Salisbury for water. I well remember the concerns of Inspector Jupp, who rode with us, that we should still have at least half a tender of water left when we passed Worting Junction; we did, and Yeovil was reached with over 1,000 gallons to spare.

Driver King and myself then worked down to Exeter before working the return train back to Waterloo, a round trip which was another first in workings over the former Southern Railway. I was also firing to driver Hooper of Nine Elms on the night he attained 105 m.p.h. with the Bulleid Pacific No. 35005 *Canadian Pacific* on the descent from Worting Junction to Winchester with the 21.20 ex-Waterloo referred to by the crews as 'The Mails'. My regular driver was Eric 'Sooty' Saunders. During my eighteen months firing to 'Sooty' numerous recordings of our runs were made, particularly when attempting to set start-to-stop times with the 17.30 Waterloo–Bournemouth of forty minutes for the Waterloo–Basingstoke section of the London South Western main line. (For a detailed account of some of these runs see 'Bournemouth Line Steam Twenty Years On' by Donald Benn in *Railway World*, vol. 48, no. 567, July 1987.)

Speaking from a fireman's perspective the most difficult work is when there is a long adverse grade, not necessarily a particularly severe one, but one which requires a sustained effort from the locomotive. An up hill and down dale type of route at least affords some respite when running the downhill stretch. The long, steady drag gives no such luxury and there are only brief respites between prolonged bouts of shovelling. If such a situation occurs in the later stages of a journey, as it would have done for fireman Wolstencroft on the footplate of *Hardwicke*, as she went over Shap, two-thirds of the way from Crewe to Carlisle, the effort becomes greater as coal has to be pulled down from the back of the tender in between the periods of shovelling. Then of course there is 'keeping the coal damped' so that the dust does not fly and spoil the driver's clean white shirt! In such situations I have known grown men argue over who would strain and then drink the two-hour-old stewed tea dregs.

Sometimes the fireman's difficulties are not produced by the route but by the locomotive, as these remarks from a ex-Patricroft driver of the London & North Western indicate:

*The hot and dirty work undertaken by the fireman is not confined to the cab. At the end of a shift the engine's smokebox would need to be emptied of the char carried through from the firebox. The fireman of 0–4–4T No. 1 of the Metropolitan Railway, built in 1896, is at work doing this very dusty job.*

When I first started firing, promotion for firemen started with the shed turner's link [shed pilot], and proceeded as for drivers, but with the advent of Whale's 'Mankillers', the drivers began to crib at having youngsters with them, as there were not even many experienced firemen who were capable of firing a '19' Goods or 'Experiment' in the normal way. They had to sling the coal in the middle of the firebox, let it coke and then spread it out with the long rake. A run down 'Precursor' could chew up coal faster than a normal fireman could shovel it in the firebox.

Talbot, The London North Western Recalled, p. 36

There can be little doubt that the various crews who competed in the 1895 races were all familiar with their locomotives and we can perhaps surmise from that that they were all competent and skilful enginemen. However, in Nock's account of the races and in his work on the locomotives of the North Eastern Railway, he gives the impression that the crews on the Great Northern were not keen to race:

Among Great Northern enginemen the race was viewed with general disquiet, the more cautious spirits definitely holding their engines in, lest they be scheduled to run at these high speeds as a regular event. . . .

There is no doubt that the Great Northern men disliked the race. They had a proud tradition of sound, economical running, and they needed the inducement of extra pay, in order to run as much ahead of time as was needed on those last nights.

Nock, Railway Races to the North, pp. 95, 97

There does seem to be something slightly amiss in these sentiments in that the Great Northern had built its reputation on the speed of its services and yet here we are presented with a view which suggests a reluctance to run at high speed. Could it be that the answer lies in the 'inducement of extra pay'? There can have been little love lost between a workforce bent on unionization and a management wholly opposed to the idea. Another hint in this direction is the remark, 'lest they be scheduled to run at these high speeds as a regular event', which it is possible to interpret as being a demotivator, for who wants to put in more effort for no extra reward? There is also a possibility that a degree or so of partiality could be clouding the assessments of the capabilities of the Great Northern's locomotives.

In his Railways of England, published in 1900, W.M. Acworth gives another clue as to why there may have been a reluctance to race, by some crews at least.

The men [top link drivers] are arranged in order of merit, that is, of economy of fuel and oil consumption, on a sheet hung up on the notice board of the running shed. Of course for a single week, extra loads or stress of wind, greasy rails or what not, may affect a man's position, but in the long run (assuming every man's engine to be in equally good condition) the man who comes out on top is the best driver, in other words, is the man who can do most work to time – for punctuality of course comes before coal saving – with the most scientific economy of force. In fact a driver feels the loss of good position on the coal sheet much as a boy feels being sent to the bottom of his form at school.

Acworth, *The Railways of England*, pp. 274–5

At this distance in time from the events it is not possible to know precisely why one company's men and machines should perform better or worse than another's. One is led to suspect ulterior and pecuniary motives; the Great Northern's footplate crews were reluctant to get involved in anything which made their working lives any more difficult until they were given a little financial reward for their extra efforts on behalf of the company's honour.

There can be little doubt that the racing was causing some controversy among the rank and file as the reported speech of John Burns MP indicates:

Mr. John Burns M.P., speaking at Battersea last night, on the occasion of the annual sports in aid of the funds of the Amalgamated Society of Railway Servants, referred to the railway race to the North. He said the drivers and firemen of fast trains were already over-taxed, while the mental and physical strain upon the guard was also very great. He had himself travelled on the footplate of engines both in America and in England, and he knew what a terrible strain there was on the mind of the driver, who had to be continually alert to see that the line was clear and that the signals were all right. If the foolish spirit of rivalry between different companies continued there was grave reason to fear that the companies' servants would suffer most seriously in health and would probably have their lives shortened.

*The Times*, 22 August 1895

Mr Burns was probably being both partial in his remarks and probably doing a bit of politicking as well, but this does not hide the fact that not all those involved with the races were totally committed. Not only are there suggestions that the Great Northern crews were reluctant racers, there are remarks which give rise to doubts about the commitment of the crews on the York–Newcastle leg.

Passing now from the North Western to the North Eastern, no time need be spent over the run of No. 1621 from York to Newcastle on the night of August 21st, when little more than strict timekeeping seems to have been attempted.

Nock, *Railway Races to the North*, p. 146

If account is taken of the way in which the men were treated over the years it is a testimony to their goodwill that they could be induced to race at all. The reluctance or otherwise exhibited by the crews is scarcely a cause for adverse comment from people for whom manual labour was undreamed of. Footplatemen

*GNR 4–2–2 Stirling 8 ft 'Single'.*

*GNR 2–2–2 Stirling 7 ft 7 in.*

*NER 4–4–0 W. Wordsdell 'M' class.*

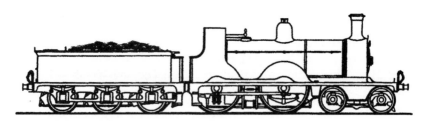

*NBR Holmes' 4–4–0.*

*Line drawings of the locomotives which took part in the races.*

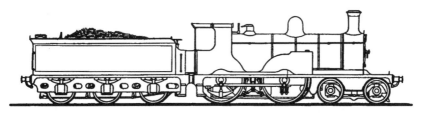

*CR Lambie's 4–4–0.*

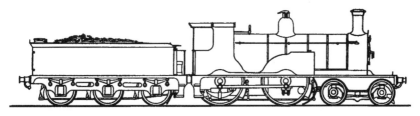

*CR Drummond's 4–4–0.*

*LNWR 'Precedent' class 2–4–0.*

*LNWR three cylinder Compound 2–2–2–0.*

were not paid to be entertainers and railway work could be demanding enough without having to put on a performance.

It is a pity that no details are available about the crews on the North British, as they carried out some excellent running, particularly on the Edinburgh–Dundee leg of the race, where they turned in a-mile-a-minute averages on this very demanding 59 mile journey. One can only surmise that in the case of the North British men the company's attitude towards union recognition did not act as a demotivating factor, or perhaps that the level of enmity towards the hated Caledonian crews was a sufficient motivator to overcome all other prejudices, although there were other aspects of the North British's performance which seem less than enthusiastic. Initially the racing train was being held to time before being allowed to depart from Edinburgh Waverley, though in the later stages of the competition this practice was rectified. Some idea of the agitation the North British's attitudes caused can be gauged from the following quote by a 'Special Correspondent' in *The Times*:

> . . . at Edinburgh there occurred an inexplicable mistake which shattered all our high hopes, and, as the results proved, led to our being thoroughly beaten into Aberdeen.
>
> 'The Race to Aberdeen', *The Times*, 21 August 1895, p. 3

It seems likely that the 'Special Correspondent' was one of the party of Rous-Marten, MacDonald, Acworth and Scott, with Rous-Marten the most likely contender.

Turning to the motive power used in the races, it was very much a cross-section of that to be found at work on the British railway network of the period. The Great Northern ran its section of the race with a combination of Stirling's locomotive types, a 7 ft 2–2–2 and the famous Stirling 8 ft 'singles' 4–2–2s. The North Eastern ran Wilson Worsdell's 4–4–0 'M1' class, nicknamed 'Rail Crushers', and the North British used the Holmes 4–4–0. 4–4–0s were also the preferred form of motive power on the Caledonian and both the Drummond 4–4–0 and Lambie's variation of it were employed. The London & North Western was represented by the 2–2–2–0 'Teutonic' class compounds and the 2–4–0 'Precedent' class, and as superheating had not yet been applied in Britain, all were saturated steam locomotives, though in subsequent years some of the locomotives in the competing classes were fitted with superheaters. The North Eastern's 'M1' class 'Rail Crusher', now at the National Railway Museum in York, has been preserved in this modified form.

A comparison of the motive power used in the races can be found in chapter five; for now it is sufficient to say that of all the performances put up during the thirty-one days of racing the least spectacular, in relative terms, are those of the Great Northern. Whether this was because of reluctance on the part of the crews or some other factor, such as the condition of the permanent way, which at the time would have been constructed using 45 ft lengths of steel rail, remains to be seen. Incidentally the lines of most main line routes were constructed in this manner, though the London & North Western was in the process of going over to what became the standard 60 ft length. The state of the Great Northern's permanent way did receive criticism at times during the 1870s and there were problems in the very early years attributed to costs and the rapidity of construction. However, there is no direct evidence that the Great Northern's permanent way was vastly inferior to that of its rivals, though the London & North Western did make publicity poster claims as to the excellence of its permanent way and make a virtue out of its punctuality.

The condition of the permanent way is certainly a factor north of Edinburgh, especially for the North British. Over the Forth in Fife, sections of the North British route to Aberdeen, between Arbroath and Montrose, were still of single line construction. The difficulty with single line working is not that the permanent way is in poor condition, but that the single line tokens need to be exchanged. Token exchange is usually performed by the fireman and it is unlikely that the exchange could take place at much above 30 m.p.h. This factor was one reason why despite a shorter overall distance the East Coast route was kept at bay by the efforts of those on the West Coast. The North British's route through Fife also suffered from having come into being through that time-honoured practice in railway circles, amalgamation, and as a result was much more of a switchback railway than the Caledonian route and hence inherently slower with its steep gradients, severe curves and proliferation of junctions, and their accompanying speed restrictions.

*During the races the North British ran over single line between Arbroath and Montrose and in doing so the fireman would have to make exchanges of the single line tokens with the signalman. When viewed like this it is easy to appreciate why the task is a difficult one to carry out when travelling at speed. The engine is William Stanier's first design for the London, Midland & Scottish Railway, a 2–6–0 mixed traffic engine, and it is seen here at Highley on the Severn Valley Railway.*

The route of the other Scottish competitor, the Caledonian, was not without its gradients – Beattock and Dunblane attest to that – but by comparison with the North British it was a route much more suited to fast running with fewer speed restrictions overall. John Soutar with engine No. 17 took the 82 miles between Stanley Junction, 7 miles out from Perth, and Ferryhill Junction on the outskirts of Aberdeen, at an average speed of 71.3 m.p.h. including a stretch of more than 11 miles at an average exceeding 75 m.p.h., well in excess of the North Eastern's '66 m.p.h. record speed' referred to by the Press Association, or *Hardwicke*'s efforts between Crewe and Carlisle.

Though the West Coast route did not have any single line sections or suffer from the difficulties created by the piecemeal development of the Edinburgh–Dundee section, it did have the more severe gradients, a severity which applied as much to length as steepness, for the East Coast route had nothing to compare with Shap or Beattock. From London to Preston on the West Coast the route was relatively easy and as far as Rugby only the climb out of Euston to Willesden could be called tough, though out as far as Tring the grade was almost continuously against the collar.

From an operating perspective the race journey on the West Coast route was divided in four sections: Euston–Crewe and Crewe–Carlisle, with both sections being run by the London & North Western, then Carlisle–Perth and Perth–Aberdeen being undertaken by Caledonian crews and locomotives. The East Coast team divided its route into five portions: King's Cross–Grantham and Grantham–York by the Great Northern, York–Newcastle and Newcastle–Edinburgh by the North Eastern, then Edinburgh–Aberdeen with North British crews and engines. In mileage terms the two longest sections were the 158 miles from Euston to Crewe and the 151 miles from Carlisle to Perth, followed by the 141 mile stretch from Crewe to Carlisle. The other distances were: Edinburgh–Aberdeen 131 miles, Newcastle–Edinburgh 124 miles, King's Cross–Grantham 105 miles, Perth–Aberdeen 90 miles, Grantham–York 82 miles, and York–Newcastle 81 miles.

The Euston–Crewe section was fitted with a set of water troughs which made the non-stop journey possible over such a distance. The Caledonian crews almost always took water at Stirling, though on one occasion during the races driver Crooks ran non-stop Carlisle–Perth. The Carlisle–Perth section, which contains the legendary climb to Beattock, was perhaps the most arduous of the sections, but Crewe–Carlisle would run a very close second. Beattock is ten miles at a gradient of 1 in 75 and close to the summit some short sections are steeper still. Offsetting this are 23 miles, mostly descending, from the summit down to Carstairs Junction. Though the run over Shap on the London & North Western is not as severely graded as Beattock its long drawn-out slog demands a longer sustained effort by both locomotive and crew to overcome it. The bonus for topping Shap was that once they had done so the crew were more or less coasting home down to Carlisle, whereas the Caledonian crew faced Beattock less than a third of the way into their journey and were still more than 100 miles from home when they crested the summit.

On the East Coast the title for most demanding section would have to be awarded to the North British, with the North Eastern coming second for its section from Newcastle to Edinburgh, but even so both of these would be behind the sections between Crewe and Perth. However, there are a great many other factors involved besides the direct comparison of gradients in any attempt to assess which was the more difficult route. The approach to a particular gradient can be as important as its severity; for instance, hitting a bank at 60 m.p.h. is a different experience altogether, in terms of keeping speed up, to hitting it at 25 m.p.h. It is this sort of difficulty which made the task of the North British crews so difficult, not that they had lots of long, hard grades, but that some of the worst ones they faced all came after speed restrictions thus preventing the enginemen making a dash at them.

Overall it would be fair to say that the West Coast route as well as being the longer of the two was also marginally more difficult from the enginemen's standpoint, for not only did they face the more sustained and severe gradients they also had the longest sections, with the exception of the Perth–Aberdeen portion. It is likewise reasonable to say that there was a slight bias, on the part of those engaged in riding with and timing the competing trains, in favour of the East Coast route in general and of Stirling's locomotives and the Great Northern in particular. Such partiality is not uncommon in railway circles and in form is comparable with the degree of rivalry which existed between the companies, with the various *aficionados* each championing their own prejudices.

Deciding to race trains was a decision taken at the highest levels. To make the race possible and secure the victory demanded the dedicated efforts of the whole company, general managers, superintendents of the line, chief locomotive engineers, district inspectors, inspectors, drivers, firemen, guards, signalmen, gangers, shunters, porters, lampmen and many others. The only available technology to control this vast army of men and resources was the telegraph and that was only available during post office opening hours. This being the case even the humble runner had his part in the race drama, scurrying to and fro between the general manager's office and the post office as the telegrams flew back and forth between Tweeddale, Conacher, Oakley, et al. Pressmen too were subject to the limitations of the existing technology and the following chapter details the way in which the press covered and recorded the events.

*Chapter Four*

# THE RACE IS ON

The relationship between the press and the railways in the Victorian era was very different from the one which exists between them in 1990s Britain. Though there were many jokes made about the railway, railwaymen and railway personalities in Victorian Britain, the railways were not the maligned and derided joke they became after the Second World War. This does not mean that the trains ran any more to time in 1895 than they do today, as these excerpts from letters to *The Times* during the racing period clearly attest.

> . . . since July 15th the East Coast train has only on nine days out of 27 arrived to time and on the remaining 18 days has been from five to 52 minutes late.
>
> 'West Coast', Letters column, *The Times*, 17 August 1895, p. 11

Four days later the following letter appeared under a nicely tongue-in-cheek subheading, 'The Race To London'. It is signed 'North East', and is a part reply to a letter from a person writing under the sobriquet 'South West'. Both South West and North East appear as parodies of the 'East Coast' and 'West Coast' appellations chosen by correspondents to the paper on the issue of the Races to the North.

> Sir, – I can confirm 'South West's' description of London and Brighton speed. I was a fellow-sufferer with him and noted exactly the time of arrival at Victoria, one hour seven minutes late.
>
> From internal evidence I am inclined to think 'South West' must be only an occasional visitant to these parts, inasmuch as he says nothing about the delay of the return train, and, indeed, appears to regard the whole transaction with surprise. We who are used to the vagaries of the 10.44 know better.
>
> 'North East', letters column, *The Times*, 21 August 1895, p. 3

Nor was that other perennial railway joke, the catering, exempted from criticism.

> I arrived the other day at Edinburgh about 6.30am., where I had about a quarter of an hour to wait. An 'express' breakfast is advertised at the

refreshment room. This was not ready. With much difficulty I persuaded a supercilious young lady to give me a cup of tea, which was not drinkable when it came, and some eggs, which must have been laid last December. At Dundee the case is even worse and complaints produce no improvement.

'A Frequent Traveller', letters column, *The Times*, 24 August 1895

Each of the routes had its champions writing to the papers, two of whom signed themselves respectively 'East Coast' and 'West Coast' and there is perhaps a hint of sarcasm in the proceedings between this pair:

. . . in his [East Coast's] eagerness to champion the route to Scotland, for which he avows his preference, has apparently entered the lists without weapons, or, in other words has neglected to provide himself with a knowledge of facts, perhaps you will kindly allow me to correct a few of the most palpable errors into which he has fallen.

'West Coast', letters column, *The Times*, 17 August 1985, p. 11

To the correspondents debating the merits and demerits of the rival routes under the banner of East Coast and West Coast we can add, for the East Coast route, one who signs himself 'E.C.J.S.', presumably East Coast Joint Stock? There is also a letter from someone who signs himself 'S.P.T.' and claims to be unbiased, though there is just a hint of partiality towards the East Coast in the tone of the letter.

In conclusion, is it out of place to ask why, with the splendid engines at their disposal – they [the LNW] are boasting of using the 'President' [Precedent] class, now about 20 years old – and Sir George Findlay knowing, as he evidently did, of what they were capable – why, I say, did not the West Coast give the public the benefit before, instead of taking the time they have done, until competition via Forth Bridge drove them to exert themselves?

'S.P.T.', letters column, *The Times*, 17 August 1895, p. 11

*The Times* and numerous other papers were themselves giving coverage to the story and *The Times*'s correspondent in Carlisle was not only giving details of arrival and departure times, but informed his editor that large crowds cheered the departure, which was at a little before one o'clock in the morning. In the 1990s the very idea that large crowds would turn out at one in the morning to watch a train departure seems ludicrous. The good burghers of Carlisle, though, were not the only ones to turn out at ungodly hours of the morning,

Early as the hour was a considerable number of people interested in the races awaited the arrival at Aberdeen, and the keenest excitement prevailed as to the result of the contest.

*Yorkshire Post*, 22 August 1895

The *Yorkshire Post* was receiving reports from or sending reporters to Crewe, York and Carlisle. In the coverage of the events on 21 August the *Yorkshire Post*'s East Coast correspondent appears to have ridden on the train, for in addition to recounting the goings-on at York he also mentioned an incident that took place during the change-over of engines at Newcastle, and that Vincent Raven himself rode the footplate on the whole York–Edinburgh section. Raven's presence does not appear to have hampered or inhibited the crew as the reporter goes on to say that,

> The train was away again [from Newcastle] two minutes afterwards, drawn by engine No. 1621 driven by Mr. G. Turner, who was evidently bent on making a record to Edinburgh, the first stop.
>
> *Yorkshire Post*, 21 August 1895

Referring to the run on the following night, with Nicholson and Blades on the footplate, O.S. Nock comments:

> despite the lateness of the hour a crowd had gathered at Berwick to see the flyer come through. At the time there was a speed restriction right down to 5mph. through the old station, but when that excited throng saw the train come tearing round the curve from Tweedmouth and up over the Royal Border Bridge they scattered for their lives.
>
> Nock, *Railway Race to the North*, p. 114

It is not only the idea that people would turn out to wave and cheer a train that seems odd, it seems equally strange that the nation's only news medium (there was no television or radio), newspapers, were sending out reporters to cover the race, and not just the local papers, but organs of the calibre of *The Times*, the *Daily Telegraph*, the *Manchester Guardian*, *The Scotsman* and the *Yorkshire Post* were all carrying reports of the race's progress. However, given the size and importance of the companies involved in the race and the fact that it involved members of the House of Lords, perhaps it should not be in the least surprising that the country's leading newspapers were sending reporters to cover the events and giving column inches as well as ample space in the letters columns to the coverage of each night's events. Nor was coverage confined to the British Isles, for the *New York Times* also gave space to the race.

> Universal interest has been aroused in the past fortnight by the prolonged race between the two chief Northern Railway lines for a record between London and Aberdeen. The competition between the east and west coast routes to this point gave rise to a great struggle in 1888, but the opening of the Forth Bridge has much altered the conditions, and this new fight has produced some extraordinary results. The east coast has some advantage in point of distance, but much heavier gradients and a rougher country [sic], so that finally it had to give in to the rival west coast route which has ultimately

performed the feat of carrying a regular passenger train of four coaches for 540 miles at an average speed of 63⅓mph. Over one section of 32 miles this side of Carlisle the speed averaged 74 m.p.h. This achievement has filled the east coast with awe and, by mutual consent, the contest has been abandoned. London papers complacently point out that no other country in the world could do such wonderful things as this. The *Daily Chronicle* does admit that very high speeds are now and then attempted on American lines, 'but everyone knows that they are risky in the last degree because of the roughness with which the lines themselves are built and kept'. No figures are obtainable here but I fancy the Empire State Express habitually and without any cackling does things quite as remarkable in their way as this wildly vaunted miracle.

'London and Politicians', *New York Times*, 25 August 1895, p. 1

This article was produced in London for the *New York Times* and before dealing with the matter of the races it was commenting on the events at Westminster. It contains one or two little inconsistencies – the east coast does not have the heavier gradients, and there seems to be little evidence to suggest a state of awe on behalf of the east coast companies; perhaps the comments of the president of the Board of Trade, C.T. Richie, came nearer to the mark when, in reply to a question from Sir John Leng, the honourable member for Dundee, as to whether or not the Board of Trade could do anything about the speed of the trains he said:

travellers must rely on the common sense of the railway companies.

*New York Times*, 24 August 1895, p. 7

There are several reasons which might be suggested for the East Coast companies' decision to stop racing: fear of the consequences if an accident were to occur, the disruption to normal operational procedures, or the inability to justify the costs to the shareholders. It may even have been common sense, but given the nature of those involved 'awe' would probably have been least of their considerations. The final sentence of the article says much about the author's attitude to the coverage of the events. The inside pages of this same edition of the *New York Times* carry an attempt at comparative analysis in an article entitled 'News of the Railroad – Comparisons between American and British Fast Trains'. This article also raises other issues which the Britons may well have contested:

It was the long continued success of the Empire State Express that gave the Britons the idea of running trains long distance at the rate of 50mph or thereabouts. The record achievement of the London North Western road in running a heavy passenger train from London to Aberdeen a distance of 540 miles in 538 minutes, although unprecedented in point of time per mile of long distance travel can scarcely be regarded as a challenge to American Railway Managers to do better. The Empire State Express has made 436½

*Locomotive No. 1, though not one of the actual race engines, is nonetheless famous, seen here with a rake of six-wheel coaching-stock of the type in use on the Great Northern at the time of the races. (National Railway Museum)*

miles in 425¾ minutes and its extraordinary running time, taking into consideration the great difference of conditions existing between British roads and the New York Central is even more remarkable than the fast time from London to Aberdeen.

*New York Times*, 24 August 1895, pp. 8–9

The article gives reasons why the New York Central road can be considered the harder and points to the speed restrictions when passing through the centre of towns (according to the article there were eight such town centre restrictions to be overcome on the journey of the Empire State Express), not as here in Great Britain separated from the highway and the storefronts, but right down the middle of the main street. The author informs us that the passage through Syracuse is in this manner, and in normal practice this section of the journey takes eight minutes, but on the occasion of Empire State Express's record time, it was undertaken in two – a truly awesome sight for the shoppers, no doubt? The article closes with a paragraph appealing to the voice of authentic authority, quoting Mr William Buchanan, who was 'Master of Motive Power' to the (naturally impartial) New York Central Railway, operators of the Empire State Express:

> William Buchanan Master of Motive Power on the New York Central system expressed the opinion the other day that the running time of the Empire State Express could be reduced by one hour with absolute safety. If such a change were made, the rate of speed would be far greater than that of the London flier which made 540 miles in 538 minutes.
>
> *New York Times*, 24 August 1895, pp. 8–9

Whatever the facts are, there is no mistaking that the efforts being made by the 'Britons' had touched a nerve. When the article's author discovered that the 540 miles were reeled off in 512 minutes and not 538 minutes, another nerve might have been struck.

The same day's paper also has a piece covering the threat to the health of the footplatemen. There were several MPs who championed the cause of the railwaymen, one was Michael Bass and another was the previously mentioned John Burns, who made speeches to the effect that the high speeds endangered the footplatemen's very sanity. The odd thing about this text is that it can be found as a letter to the *Daily Telegraph*, which is quoted in the *Manchester Guardian*, also on 24 August.

In his remarks on the racing Burns was of the opinion that the races would 'strain' the driver's mind and he had 'reason to fear for the men's health'. The repudiation of this view was provided, as far as can be ascertained, by an engine-driver, formerly of the Great Northern railway, but at the time of writing employed in America on the New York Central Railway. The engine-driver wrote to the *Daily Telegraph* putting the footplate perspective, or one of them. He began by saying, 'I am very much amused by the remarks made by Mr. John Burns M.P.', and continues with:

> During my service as an engineer [an American term, equivalent to the British engine-driver] I have driven the fastest trains on the Great Northern Railway and on the New York Central railway. On the latter road I regularly drove the Empire State Express, at that time the fastest train in the world. I think, therefore, that I may with justice claim to know as much about fast trains as Mr. John Burns M.P. Mr. Burns, if he is correctly reported, says 'He had travelled thousands of miles on the footplate across the prairie when the engine was spinning away at the rate of sixty or seventy miles an hour and therefore knew what it was [to travel at speed].'
>
> 'An Express Driver', letter to the *Daily Telegraph*,
> from the *Manchester Guardian*, 24 August 1895, p. 8

The engine-driver goes on to inform his readers that not only are footplate rides forbidden in the United States, but that none of the prairie railroads, which are all west of Chicago, travel at speeds anything like 70 m.p.h., due in the main to the lightly laid rail and, mostly, single track. On the issue of footplate access he says:

> I cannot believe that the officials of any American road, considering the trouble they have had with Socialists, would give Mr. John Burns M.P. an order to ride on an engine.
>
> 'An Express Driver', letter to the *Daily Telegraph*,
> from the *Manchester Guardian*, 24 August 1895, p. 8

The interesting point about this incident is that here is an engineman in the United States, an expatriate, following the races from over 3,000 miles away, sending a letter to the *Daily Telegraph* where it is printed, and other newspapers find the letter interesting enough to copy and, in the case of the *New York Times*, to incorporate it within an article. This is a sequence of events which seems highly improbable in the relationship between newspapers, railwaymen and railways in the 1990s.

The newspaper in late Victorian Britain took rather a different format from that which we are used to today. The first and most notable difference was that the front page did not carry the headlines of the major news story of the day, but mostly small advertisements. This factor alone makes it rather difficult to assess the degree of importance attached to the races, and there were also major differences in layout, type sizes, for both headlining and text, and an absence of photographs, though there were some drawings. However, despite these drawbacks to a direct comparison, it is possible to assess the size of the coverage in relation to other events of the day and in relation to the number of, and space given to, letters to the editor connected with the races, as opposed to the other issues of the day, which should be of some help in assessing the importance attached to the events.

On Wednesday 14 August 1895 *The Times* carried the reports of the half-yearly general meetings of the London & North Western Railway, the Maryport & Carlisle Railway, and the Merthyr Tydfil Junction Railway – the space in the London & North Western's reportage given over to the races was greater than the coverage given to both of the other railways half-yearly meetings, and represented 25 per cent of the coverage of the London & North Western's meeting. On 17 August two entire columns of letters to the editor concerned the races, and included tables of arrival times. On 21 August, on page three (the first page of news coverage), one and a half columns were given over to an article on the race by the paper's 'Special Correspondent'.

The article by the Special Correspondent is set alongside a half-column devoted to the America's Cup races, the other half of which carried news items on Morocco, Ecuador, Turkey, Abyssinia (Ethiopia), Australia, China and South Africa, on topics such as rail strikes, strife between Italy and Abyssinia and the continuing unrest between missionaries and the Chinese. The following day, 22 August, the race coverage was again greater than that afforded the trouble in Abyssinia. Further coverage was given on the 23rd and 24th with that on the 24th giving a table of arrival times of the two routes at Aberdeen for the whole period from 29 July to 22 August.

The coverage given by the other leading papers was scarcely less, the *Manchester Guardian* report on 24 August ran to over a column and there had previously been a half-column on the 21st and an article on the 22nd. The coverage given, which, as mentioned earlier, was described by Nock as 'sensational', does not seem so by the standards common in the 1990s, indeed the reporting confines itself very much to the facts. Though there is some speculative disquiet about the speeds, it amounts to very little in comparison with the total of coverage given and where the issue of speed is raised, it is not without qualifications.

> With respect to the complaint that rapid travelling causes a sensation of nausea, it may be mentioned that the officials at Euston have received from a passenger who travelled on Tuesday night's express a telegram saying the progress of the train was so smooth and comfortable that the occupants could hardly realise the fact they were travelling at a higher rate of speed than by an ordinary train.
>
> 'Own Correspondent', *The Times*, 22 August 1895, p. 3

There is of course a possibility that the telegram referred to is that which Nock tells us was sent by Sir Edward Watkin, which would make the comments less than objective. However, the newspaper reader would not be aware of these facts and thus the point I wished to make is not altered by that knowledge.

Still on the subject of speed, Nock in his *Railway Race to the North* provides a quote from a gentleman from Elgin who had answered Nock's call for first-hand information, put out in the railway magazines during his researches in the mid-1950s.

> I remember the stern comments of some of the grave and revered seniors, who were appalled that such dangerous goings-on should be allowed. I remember one pleasing tale of an old gentleman we knew who was going north by Perth. The driver must have been feeling his oats. Anyhow, coming down from Crieff Junction (now, of course, Gleneagles) the train started to shift a bit. This got on the old boy's nerves. After a while he could stand it no longer, and in the face of threatened penalties he decided to pull the communication cord. However at that time the communication cord only functioned on the right hand side of the compartment facing the direction of travel. There might be a cord on the left hand side, and often was, but it was not connected up. In his agitation the old boy got hold of the wrong cord. He pulled and pulled until he got to the end of the rope, and then gave up in despair. He arrived at the north end of the tunnel in a state of tremendous agitation with his compartment festooned with communication cord. He confided his woes to the ticket collector at Perth, and all the consolation he got was to be told that he was adjectively lucky it had happened that way or else he would have been fined five pounds.
>
> Nock, *Railway Race to the North*, p. 84

The headlines to the articles and letters in *The Times* and the *Manchester Guardian* referred either to the 'Race to Scotland' or the 'Race to Aberdeen', the *Yorkshire Post* had 'Great Railway Race' over the subheading, 'A World's Record Established'. Another was 'The Great Race to Scotland', with subheadings 'Records Again Broken' and 'A Victory for the East Coast Companies', hardly sensational. The headlines were single column width and by 1990s standards the type size would be no more than that used in subheadings at best. By the standards of the day they appear neither bolder nor lesser than the others surrounding them, making it difficult to decide if the reportage was sensationalist. There is little doubt that the coverage was extensive, and that it was sustained over a lengthy period of time, but whether this amounts to sensationalism is another matter.

The articles sent in under the name 'Special Correspondent' were accurate and informed, beginning with a résumé of the contest of 1888 and raising the issue of the record of the Empire State Express. They were also at times a little tongue-in-cheek:

> How our great companies come to be running trains at these marvellous speeds it is difficult to say. The public has jumped to the conclusion that they are racing each other. But this explanation must be wrong, for Lord Stalbridge, who, as Chairman of the North Western, surely must know, has assured his shareholders that there is no such thing as racing, though it is true that he afterwards added that the North Western would not be last in the race.

> 'Special Correspondent', *The Times*, 21 August 1895, p. 3

The quality and accuracy of the newspapers' coverage was given a further boost by the remarks contained in a letter sent by Henry Conacher to Sir Henry Oakley following the West Coast's run on 22/23 August.

> I have been comparing their run with ours as described in the newspapers with a view to seeing exactly how they were able to run 17 miles [more] in eight minutes less time, and have put the comparison on [*sic*] the form of the Table annexed.

> Nock, *Railway Race to the North*, p. 123

The coverage given by the *Yorkshire Post* was perhaps the most fulsome, but even here it is difficult to describe the coverage as being particularly sensational, the following being typical of the least strictly objective pieces – though even here one would hesitate to use the term sensationalism.

> Neither of the competing groups of companies show the least disposition to yield the palm to its rival, and the breaking of records on one route only strengthens the determination of the officials on the other to eclipse all previous achievements.

> *Yorkshire Post*, 23 August 1895, p. 5

This article covers almost three columns and includes quotes from railway officials, times of departure and arrival, records of intermediate speeds; today this article would be seen as one for 'trainspotters' not headline news.

Euston Station was the scene of much excitement about eight o'clock last night, a considerable number of spectators having arrived to give the West Coast train a 'send off'. The officials were determined if possible to wipe out the defeat sustained on the previous night, when their rivals won by 15 minutes. The train consisted of three large bogie carriages, which were fairly well filled with passengers, some of whom were visibly suffering from suppressed excitement, as though on the eve of doing great things. The driver of the train had received instructions to make the best time possible, and one facetious youth who was seeing a party of friends off seized upon it as the basis for some lugubrious predictions, and an earnest appeal to take insurance tickets.

*Yorkshire Post*, 23 August 1895, p. 5

The bulk of the coverage and debates, at least those being carried on in the letters columns of the newspapers, were not so much about late arrivals, excessive speeds or the quality of the catering, as about the composition of the trains, and the stations for which passengers would be carried. The essentials of the letters and reportage are that the East Coast ran with more coaches, though they were smaller and lighter than their West Coast comparisons, and that they carried passengers to more intermediate destinations than the West Coast team.

Surprisingly the official figures for through-passengers show that they were relatively few in number. On 2 July, just prior to the races, the East Coast train carried 75 passengers and the West Coast carried 25. Between 19 and 21 August the East Coast carried 101 and the West Coast 35, and on the night of 22 August the figures were 34 and 10 respectively. It would be hard to describe these figures as healthy, though it must be remembered that both routes were running regular trains, carrying the bulk of the traffic, behind the racing trains. The odd thing about the figures is that they do not seem to match the 'well filled with passengers' remark in the report by the *Yorkshire Post*, quoted above.

The disruption to traffic and the necessity to run additional services led the North British management to extract assurances from both the North Eastern and the Great Northern indemnifying them against any losses incurred through the running of a service in a less than normal service pattern. However, indemnities or not *The Scotsman* reported the race's progress from Edinburgh in fine style, and there are some indications that though only thirty people rode from King's Cross, some passengers joined the train either in Edinburgh or Dundee.

The English companies had done their bit splendidly; it remained for the North British Railway to maintain at least what had been handed on to them. This they easily did, and more. It took thirteen minutes to do the nine miles and a half between Edinburgh and Dalmeny; but after this a mile a minute and more was the order of the night. The train went over the bridge [Forth

Bridge] in a minute and fifteen seconds, and romped away through Fife in a most satisfactory manner. Its rush was such that it was very difficult, even sitting at an open window, and eagerly watching, to make out the stations as the train flew past them, but there was no check, and good work was maintained. Burntisland was passed at 2.42am, twelve minutes to the good; two minutes were dropped on the run to Ladybank, there being a stiffish incline at Falkland Road. At Leuchars the express was eleven minutes to the good; the Tay Bridge was crossed in less than two minutes, and amid the cheers of a large crowd of people the train steamed into Dundee Station at 3.20am, twelve minutes before the scheduled time.

*The Scotsman*, from the *Manchester Guardian*, 24 August 1895, p. 8

During the final days of the races there was a collision in the English Channel between the ferries *Seaford* and *Lyon*, in which the *Seaford* was lost and the *Lyon* rescued 'hundreds of people who were in danger'. The reportage of the race and the disaster at sea in both *The Times* and the *Manchester Guardian* were given almost equal space and the accounts appeared together on the same page. The prominence given to the race in such circumstances may seem a little callous to some, but if the degree of importance enjoyed by the railways is taken into account it does mitigate this slightly. For instance the financial reports in the papers of the 1890s are usually headed 'Railway and other company Reports', again demonstrating the importance of the railway up to that point, in the financial as well as commercial life of the country.

Turning to the more specialist press, two substantial articles, written by Rous-Marten, appeared in *The Engineer* and were accompanied by numerous letters to the editor, one of which was from Rous-Marten himself. The reporting of the race was not as accurate, at times, as it might have been and Rous-Marten had been given details about events on the West Coast which were quite simply wrong; worse still he had written the error into his article in *The Engineer*, hence the letter, which was to put matters straight. Rous-Marten's correspondent had informed him, wrongly, that the Caledonian 'single' No. 123 had worked the West Coast train forward from Stirling on the morning of 23 August. This was wrong on both counts – No. 123 was not used and the engine change took place as usual at Perth; the actual locomotive was the Lambie 4–4–0 No. 17 with driver Soutar and fireman Fenton on the footplate.

This incident aside, the coverage afforded to the races was, in general terms, relatively accurate. Equally one would be forced to admit that the reportage does not appear to be especially sensationalist, at least not in *The Scotsman*, *The Times*, *Manchester Guardian* or *Yorkshire Post* articles. Headlines are not spread across the whole front page, and are no more than a single column wide and though the coverage is prominent and fairly extensive it is not written in a manner that would make one hesitate to ride on one of the race trains. The coverage of the Channel collision is far racier:

Deafened by the crash of splintered planks and shattered glass which accompanied the concussion, I turned quickly round, and saw a few yards off our port side a steamer with an enormous hole, like a gigantic bite taken out of her bows. From the top of her stern almost to the waterline her plates were crumpled up and burst in. As for the Seaford she was in more woeful plight.

'Eye witness account', *Daily Telegraph*,
from the *Manchester Guardian*, 22 August 1895, p. 5

The nearest the papers come to sensationalizing the races is perhaps in these remarks from the *Manchester Guardian*:

Mile a minute travelling is certainly not a sedative to nervous people; but to the mentally and physically sound there is something very exhilarating in such rapid travelling even in the dead of night when all forms, as the train flies past them, blend without outline in the general gloom. Those who saw the train rushing through the country in the darkness of the night describe it as, 'like a flash of wildfire'.

*Manchester Guardian*, 24 August 1895, p. 8

Whether or not the reporting was sensational, there can be no denying the interest of the general public, not only for newspaper coverage but in actually turning out to watch the racing trains.

On the last night's racing the final leg of the West Coast's race route, that between Perth and Aberdeen, was in the hands of driver Soutar and fireman Fenton and *The Sketch* recorded their entry into Aberdeen:

Driver Soutar, who has all along been in charge of this engine [the Lambie 4–4–0 No. 17], is the railway hero of the moment. Soutar, who is nearly sixty-one, joined the service as a fireman forty-four years ago. He has conveyed the Queen to the North on many occasions with this very engine. There was much excitement at Aberdeen on the great day, the train being waited for by a crowd of spectators. Soutar and his stoker were borne shoulder-high and presented with a couple of blue ribbons. A unique result of the race was that letters which left London by the eight o'clock evening train were sent out in Aberdeen on the first morning delivery.

Nock, *Railway Race to the North*, p. 121

Another recurring theme throughout the coverage is that the events were a public spectacle, with crowds being present at stations en route or individuals watching the trains race by their chosen vantage points.

. . . and C.J. Alcock has told me of the amazing sight she [No. 1309 *Adriatic*] made from the old L.N.W.R. station at Chalk Farm. A thunderstorm of terrifying intensity was raging over London, one of the worst Alcock remembers in his long life of eighty years; the torrential rain, the showers of sparks from the engine, the flashes of lightning that lit up that gleaming black compound and her three coaches as she came blazing up Camden bank set a note of high drama as the 'flyer' swept by and plunged into Primrose Hill tunnel.

Nock, Railway Race to the North, p. 119

The specialist railway journal, *Railway Times*, not only dealt with the races at the time but, later in the year in October, offered its readership details on how the races affected the services to Braemar, Elgin, Peterhead and Inverness, which saw journey times reduced by amounts of between 45 minutes and 130 minutes. The same article continued by explaining that these improvements had also led to the East Coast companies competing for the Glasgow traffic, and actually running a service that was 30 minutes faster than the West Coast's time. The West Coast responded in predictable fashion by introducing its own acceleration and a brand new service – the 11.50 a.m. ex-Euston calling at Crewe, Carlisle and Glasgow and covering the 401 miles in 8 hours. One week earlier the same journal had a comparative analysis style article similar in nature to the one referred to in the *New York Times*.

This article, being in a publication that was more interested in the financial and managerial aspects of railway working, contains not only details of the average speeds and top speeds, but also the information that the Empire State Express was reputed to be earning about US $90,000 per month, more than one million dollars a year – a tidy sum from one train.

All sections of the social spectrum from lords to clergymen and engine-drivers had a part in the races, and a not inconsiderable proportion of the general public showed a great deal of interest in the proceedings. It would be very interesting to see public reaction if a similar form of event were to be organized and reported on television in the news, and in current events programmes today.

The 'Great Railway Races' were given a second airing in the mid-1950s in a series of articles in the *British Railways Staff Magazine*. It is possible that these articles were the inspiration behind the request made to O.S. Nock, by Ian Allan and G. Freeman Allen, to write a book on the races. What is certain is that shortly after these articles were published Nock did begin his researches for *The Railway Race to the North* and the first edition was published in 1958. The articles in question appeared in 1954, under the pen name 'Scot', and in the second instalment 'Scot' says,

Due to publicity given by the press, a large crowd gathered at the Great Northern railway, Kings Cross station, on the night of July 22nd to watch the departure of the 8pm east coast express to the north, a rumour being whispered the while that an effort would be made to establish a record run.

'Scot', 'Our Story', British Railways Staff Magazine, p. 29

'Scot' concludes his articles with a brief look at the merits and demerits of racing trains:

As a benefit to the travelling public, these accelerated night services had latterly become worthless and all that seems to have been derived was the

*The Victorian railway business was well aware of the values of publicity and the picture postcard was one of the means used to publicize them. One of the Holmes 4–4–0s is at work with a train of very similar proportions to those utilized in the racing on the North British. This reproduction is taken from a postcard issued by the North British at the turn of the century. (National Railway Museum)*

discomfort of having to disembark at some thoroughly inconvenient hour when welcome would hardly be in order.

> 'Scot', 'Our Story', *British Railways Staff Magazine*, p. 190

Half a century earlier, *The Engineer* closed its article on the races with the comment,

> One gratifying result of the race will be perhaps to silence the boasting of the American press. The far famed Empire State Express has been thoroughly beaten . . .

> Nock, *Railway Race to the North*, p. 128

The impression that what had been a trans-Atlantic public spectacle in 1895 had become, by the 1950s, an in-house topic for a railwayman's magazine and merely a matter of obscure interest to railway historians, could well be contradicted by references in an article written by Matthew Engel in *The Guardian* of 28 December 1994:

For the middle-classes there were all sorts of possibilities. Eating out was becoming popular in places recognisable as modern restaurants rather than dimly-lit chop houses. It was possible to stay in a first-class hotel for half a crown a night. Trains raced from London to Aberdeen in eight and a half hours (rather slower if they were not racing). It was a brief, glorious interlude when swift, safe and reasonably comfortable travel was possible but the air was not yet filled with exhaust fumes.

Engel, M., '1895 and All That', The Guardian, 28 December 1994, p. 3

The railway's position both socially and industrially was very different in late Victorian Britain from its position as the twenty-first century approaches, and this complicates the assessment of media interest in the events and the reactions of the public to them. There is an air bordering on nostalgia in the remarks made by Engel in his article, particularly in the final sentence. Naturally this aspect is missing in the contemporaneous reportage. There is, perhaps, a touch of lionizing, particularly of the enginemen in the Victorian newspaper coverage, and an element of triumphant nationalism on both sides of the Atlantic in references to the performances of the American railway company's operation of the Empire State Express and the setting of records in Britain.

*Chapter Five*

# OFF AND RUNNING

This chapter covers the performances and details of the racing, with a mix of direct personal experience in dealing with assessments of the crews' performances, and the work of Charles Rous-Marten and O.S. Nock in assessing the locomotive performances. The detailed logs used in this chapter are broadly based on those provided by Nock in his *Railway Race to the North*, which he, in turn, had constructed from the work of Rous-Marten, N.D. MacDonald, W.J. Scott and, in certain cases, company records of passing times at the signal-boxes along the routes. Further details are provided by a figure whom Nock describes as,

> a certain W.M. Lellan, who appears to have been a North British headquarters' man sent out to snoop.

> Nock, *Railway Race to the North*, p. 137

John Thomas, in his book on the North British, informs his readers that General Inspector W. McLellan rode on the footplate of the North British race train on the night of 21/22 August, and that by good fortune on the following day he was in a position to gain details of the performance of the Caledonian crew. The circumstances were that on 23 August, McLellan was visiting Fort William, to attend a Board of Trade enquiry into a derailment. The Board of Trade's inspector, according to Thomas, already had a copy of the Caledonian's running times and allowed McLellan to copy them. This was how Conacher managed to have a copy of the Caledonian's times in less than twenty-four hours after the race had been run.

Initially, McLellan had been instructed by Conacher to ride on the footplate of the North British engine and then furnish Conacher with a report of all that happened, and thus McLellan would be well aware of the importance, to Conacher, of having the Caledonian's figures at the earliest possible opportunity. McLellan's report to Conacher seems to suggest that details of the timings exist for the run to Aberdeen on the night of 21/22 August, though they do not appear to be the ones used by Nock as the source for times in his re-creation of the North British's run from Edinburgh to Dundee.

> Speed as you will see from the statement of today's running was very high and the restrictions through Junctions and over the Tay Bridge and picking

up and leaving tablets were pretty well put aside, and my opinion is we cannot improve upon it.

One minute and fifty seconds over the Forth Bridge and one minute and forty seconds over the Tay Bridge was very sharp work, and I heard a gentleman complain of the excessive speed at which the train was run to our Aberdeen agent.

Thomas, *The North British Railway*, vol. 2, p. 53

When discussing the workings undertaken by the North British, Nock says:

The running of engine No. 293 in the early hours of August 22nd has been the most difficult to 'reconstruct' of any. Those who travelled by the East Coast trains north of Edinburgh have left us no clues as to the details of the work; there is no mention of whether the curves were taken fast or slow, no comments on the discomfort, or otherwise. The times handed down to us are those at Dalmeny, Kirkcaldy, Thornton and Leuchars; the rest can be no more than conjecture, but I have attempted a reconstruction on the basis that the Forth Bridge was crossed at about 50 to 52mph.

Nock, *Railway Race to the North*, p. 149

The 1 minute and 50 seconds timing for crossing the Forth Bridge in McLellan's report is very close to Nock's estimated speed of 50 to 52 m.p.h. However, the time of 1 minute and 40 seconds for crossing the Tay Bridge is a little higher than Nock's estimate of 60 m.p.h., which would give a crossing time of around 2 minutes and 20 seconds. McLellan was not understating matters if 1 minute and 40 seconds was the time for the Tay Bridge crossing, when he says it was 'very sharp work' – indeed it was.

It seems entirely possible, even probable, that O.S. Nock's W.M. Lellan is one and the same person as Thomas's Inspector W. McLellan, particularly as both appear to work for the North British and fulfil a similar role in both narratives – that of providing Conacher with details of the performance of the Caledonian. Thomas's quote from McLellan's report to Conacher on the North British's performance also hints that there are more details of the timings of the run other than the times given for covering the Tay and Forth Bridges, though the degree of accuracy may be open to doubt.

Whatever the intervening speeds and timings were between Edinburgh and Dundee there seems little dispute over departure and arrival times and the mile-a-minute average for the whole journey, a quite remarkable performance by any standards.

For a great many people, both then and now, the Races to the North are about the heroics of the footplatemen, the speeds and the feats of enginemanship which enliven the contest and the logs both reconstructed and actual are a part of the explanation of those deeds. In purely romantic terms they may be right. The glow from the fire as the fireman shovels, illuminating the steam, smoke and sparks flying from the chimney top, the harsh bark of the exhaust as the gradients of

Beattock, Shap and Dunblane are attacked, and the hustle and bustle of changing engines at York or Crewe in front of an excited and cheering crowd. These are some of the images of steam locomotives racing through the night, over hundreds of miles, which the title the Railway Races to the North conjures up. The question is, how far do these pictures distort the reality of the situation; perhaps even the idea of romance itself is questionable in such circumstances?

Having had the benefits, if that they be, of experiencing both a romantic view of footplate life and work, and the actual reality of it as a daily employment, I can comment not only from a standpoint of romance, but from the theory and practice of footplate life. The theory tells you that each locomotive of the same design is the same as every other locomotive built to that design. The practical experience of different locomotives of the same class is that though all members of the class are broadly similar, no two are alike. To give an example from my own railway work, the 'Merchant Navy' class locomotives Nos 35004 *Cunard White Star* and 35013 *Blue Funnel* were in theory and appearance identical, yet to make No. 35004 *Cunard White Star* steam, firing had to follow the textbook – a light bright fire, with firing to the brightest spots at regular intervals. No. 35013 *Blue Funnel*, on the other hand could be fired with a wheelbarrow and plank: so long as you kept on tipping the coal into the firebox, she would steam.

The reason for raising these issues is to illustrate the sort of difficulties to be overcome in attempting to assess the performances of the crews without some knowledge of the real, as opposed to romantic, notions of footplate work. In conducting the research for this book I have been a frequent visitor to the National Railway Museum in York, where the locomotive No. 790 *Hardwicke* is kept. When I look at the dimensions and at the footplate of this locomotive it seems to me incredible that this was the locomotive which did more duties and created more records than any of the others used during the race period. I try to put the 141 miles between Crewe and Carlisle, including the climb over Shap, on *Hardwicke*'s footplate, alongside my own firing experiences on the Waterloo–Bournemouth service. This service took two hours for the 108 mile journey stopping at Basingstoke, Winchester, Southampton and Brockenhurst with one of Bulleid's Pacifics, and I find myself wondering at the differences between my efforts and those of fireman Wolstencroft as 141 miles were covered in 126 minutes, without a break.

Those whose background is in engineering will produce indicated horsepower figures, talk in pounds per mile of coal consumed or gallons of water evaporated, but will that tell you anything about fireman Wolstencroft's efforts, or my own come to that? I think not. The engineer would say that No. 790 *Hardwicke*, with a heating surface of such a size, a grate area of so many square feet, could produce steam at a rate of so many pounds per hour, but this would still not tell us anything about fireman Wolstencroft's performance. Personal direct experience of the fireman's duties informs, and common sense indicates that Wolstencroft would be hard at work, but not when, where or how he would be working, nor what sort of techniques were being employed in driving and firing *Hardwicke*, and there are several ways of driving or firing – which ones to use and at what times were a matter of experience.

The technique being used to drive the locomotive affects the way in which the fireman needs to perform his duties. For instance, some drivers would shorten the cut-off (the length of time the valves are open, admitting steam to the cylinder) to a point where there would not be sufficient draught created to keep a thick fire properly supplied with air. If this happened the fire would begin to look dead and dull, being starved of oxygen, and the fireman would have to use the fire-irons, namely the dart, to poke the fire about to get air through it. Trying to manoeuvre an 8–9 ft long steel poker within the confines of the locomotive footplate is no fun, especially if the engine is travelling at speed and particularly when trying to put it away after use, when it is very, very hot. There are many other ways in which steaming troubles can occur, but what they all illustrate is the need for the footplate crew to work as a team.

With a free-steaming locomotive, good coal and a good driver, the fireman's work would be considerably less arduous than if the engine was not steaming well, the tender was loaded with poor grade coal and the driver was making no effort to minimize the engine's poor steaming by altering his method of driving accordingly. What it is possible to say about fireman Wolstencroft's efforts is that by the time No. 790 *Hardwicke* was being asked to produce maximum effort, on the climb from Carnforth to Shap summit, 78 of the 141 miles had been travelled, and coal would need pulling down from the back of the tender to the shovelling plate, thus increasing the effort Wolstencroft would have to make. By comparison, fireman Smith would have still had plenty of coal at the shovelling plate as he and driver Crooks began their journey over Beattock which, though being steeper than Shap, is considerably earlier in the turn of duty when both engine and crew are still fresh. The climb to Beattock summit is almost continuous on leaving Carlisle, at gradients of approximately 1 in 220, with the steepest stretch between Beattock station and Beattock summit occurring 40 miles into Crooks's and Smith's turn of duty.

The most that can be said of the individual efforts of the racing crews is that they must all have been of a very high standard, for unless boiler pressure is maintained in excess of 80 per cent of the design maximum, it is highly unlikely that the locomotive will be capable of delivering the type of performance needed to achieve the speeds and reliability seen in the races. The degree of reliability exhibited between 16 July and 23 August by the West Coast route was remarkable, achieving the phenomenal figures of thirty early arrivals and only four late ones. The figures for the East Coast services by comparison show two arrivals on time and thirteen early, the remaining nineteen services were late. Crude though these figures are, they do nothing to detract from the remarkable record of the London & North Western/Caledonian partnership.

The capability and motivation of the crews can only be a matter of speculation, except where the crews themselves have commented or their actions cannot be interpreted in any other manner. Previous chapters have given details of the working conditions of the footplatemen, which can really only be described as harsh by modern standards, and there is no lack of evidence of friction between the men and the management over pay and working conditions. However, in most cases it does seem that the race trains were worked by crews who were enthusiastic and committed, irrespective of any grievances that may have existed. There are some comments which seem to suggest that not all the North Eastern crews on the York–Newcastle leg were putting in their best efforts.

Before dismissing the efforts of these crews there is, of course, the view that if an arrival time has been given then the skilful engineman arrives on time, having used the minimum amount of effort to achieve that end. It might have been that the driver on the York–Newcastle section was a man who worked in this manner, and in his way he would be correct if he asserted that his was the best performance. However, this type of running was not the spirit of the event and as such there is a hint of 'dismissal' in Nock's comments on the work of one of these crews:

> Passing now from the North Western to the North Eastern, no time need be spent over the run of No. 1621 from York to Newcastle on the night of August 21st, when little more than strict timekeeping seems to have been attempted.
>
> Nock, *Railway Race to the North*, p. 146

Though the actions of the York to Newcastle crew were not as 'devil may care' as those of some of the others, running strictly to time requires more in the way of attention to detail by the driver than simply giving the locomotive her head. This being the case it undoubtedly requires higher degrees of enginemanship, and the log of this run ought, perhaps, to have been included on those grounds, even if the actual performance did not enter into the spirit of events. However, the attention to detail required in running to the timetable is nowhere near as demanding as the efforts required to run the Carlisle–Perth leg non-stop, as Archibald Crooks and Robert Smith did.

In making assessments of the enginemanship involved in the locomotive workings, there are numerous considerations. A critical factor, particularly for the longer sections, was water use and water capacity. The London & North Western was able to run the 158 miles from Euston to Crewe and the 141 miles from Crewe to Carlisle non-stop because of their use of the water trough. The water trough had been designed and installed on the London & North Western by their chief mechanical engineer, John Ramsbottom, as early as 1860. The water-filled troughs were set between the rails and accessed by a scoop mounted beneath the tender, which was lowered into the trough by the fireman. The forward motion of

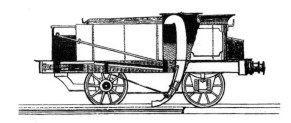

*LNWR tender showing 'scoop' arrangement.*

*The 'secret weapon', the water troughs, which allowed the London North Western to run long distances non-stop. Here 'Precedent' 2–4–0 No. 868* Condor *is making full use of the facility. (National Railway Museum)*

the locomotive forced the water up through the scoop and the pipe to which it was connected and thence into the tender. The only railways that did not eventually use the scoop and trough method were those which came to form the Southern Railway. However, at the time of the races, the only competing company to use them was the London & North Western.

It was previously mentioned that on one occasion a Caledonian train was worked non-stop from Carlisle to Perth, without the usual stop at Stirling for water. This particular run was made by driver Crooks and fireman Smith with the Drummond 4–4–0 No. 90 and, as events transpired, it was also the final night's racing. The distance from Carlisle to Perth is 150.8 miles and No. 90's tender held 3,572 gallons; to cover the 151 miles on the available water capacity meant that consumption could not exceed 24 gallons per mile. To put this into some kind of perspective,

the Caledonian had tenders with a water capacity of 3,572 gallons, so that a non-stop run from Carlisle to Stirling needed the most expert of enginemanship if the going was to be hard between Carlisle and Beattock Summit.

Nock, *Railway Race to the North*, p. 135

There is a little qualification which needs to be made: in the above quote Nock is referring to running with a much heavier load than Crooks was handling. However, in Crooks's favour, Perth is 33 miles beyond Stirling or 825 gallons of water away at 25 gallons per mile, though that is a very low rate – Nock mentions 30 gallons as being good.

If the prize for best performance throughout the races is awarded on the basis of the most skilfully demanding piece of enginemanship, then driver Archibald Crooks and his fireman Robert Smith would be very strong contenders, though the margin of their victory was but a hair's breadth from disaster:

> . . . J.F. McEwan told how the engine had to be nursed in from Auchterarder and how they arrived in Perth with the tender tank absolutely dry. In such straits were Crooks and his mate that they uncoupled, ran ahead, and just waited for a pull to the shed.
>
> Nock, *Railway Race to the North*, p. 137

In attempting this sort of running it is not only the skill of the driver in handling the engine that counts, the fireman must do everything possible to avoid wasting water and, at the same time, maintain full steam pressure. The two most common ways in which water is wasted are through blowing off excess steam pressure via the safety valves and in turning the injectors on and off. Preventing blowing off while coincidentally maintaining maximum boiler pressure is not the easiest of tasks. Fireman Smith must have been very much on top of his trade for driver Crooks even to contemplate undertaking such a run, and both boiler and tender would have needed to be full to the top before leaving Carlisle station.

The debate over which crew or locomotive put up the best performance will never go away – why should it, when for many it provides entertainment? What is certain is that the races did test the crews and their locomotives to the limits of their abilities.

A purist might well wish to champion the work of Crooks and Smith on the basis of the economy with which they achieved their run. On the other hand, those who believe that high speed is the measure could be inclined to support the cause of driver John Soutar and his mate fireman David Fenton for their efforts in running at a 75 m.p.h. average for over 11 miles between Coupar Angus and Glamis. This pairing is further credited with speeds in excess of 80 m.p.h. on the section between Stonehaven and Ferryhill Junction on the outskirts of Aberdeen. The highest average speeds in the races on the East Coast route belong to the North Eastern Railway, through the efforts of the Gateshead crew of driver Bob Nicholson and fireman Tom Blades with the Worsdell 'M1' class 4–4–0 No. 1620. No. 1620 recorded an average of 78.8 m.p.h. for the 5 mile section between Drem and Longniddry and this rose to 81.0 m.p.h. over the 2.7 miles between Cocksburnspath and Innerwick. Nicholson and Blades covered the 75 miles from Longhirst to Dunbar with No. 1620 at an average of 67.3 m.p.h. Of all the racing trains only engine No. 790 *Hardwicke* achieved higher long-distance average speeds than these.

On the night of 22/23 August No. 790 *Hardwicke* covered the 8.2 miles between Plumpton and Wreay at an average speed of 82 m.p.h. and covered the

73.4 miles between Minshull Vernon and Carnforth at an average of 68.3 m.p.h. These are the best figures throughout the whole race period and they make the figures for the Great Northern seem slow by comparison. The highest Great Northern average is that of 74.2 m.p.h. over the 12.2 miles from Hitchin to Sandy.

Despite all these competing claims, each of which has its own particular merits, in my estimation the award for finest performance of the whole race must go to the Crewe driver Ben Robinson and his stoker, fireman Wolstencroft, for their efforts from Crewe to Carlisle with No. 790 *Hardwicke* on the night of 22/23 August. The 'jewel in the crown' of this performance has to be the 62.4 m.p.h. average between Carnforth and Shap summit, which is 31.5 miles uphill over an average gradient of 1 in 188. On the East Coast, to add to the fine efforts of Nicholson and Blades, there should be mentioned the runs made by the North British crews on the Edinburgh–Dundee section. Though the average speed for this run was only marginally over 60 m.p.h. the nature of the route is such that this represents an extremely fine piece of work by the crew.

> . . . the North British running between Edinburgh and Dundee stands completely apart. Since the end of World War I there has not been any train over this stretch making a non-stop run in less than 80 minutes.
>
> Nock, *Railway Race to the North*, p. 149

The performance by the crews on the North Eastern was described as 'variable', with some putting in no more effort than was required to keep time, while others like Nicholson and Blades went at their work with gusto. The Great Northern, though possessing a reputation as being the fastest railway in the country, did not put up the fastest speeds. Most of the accelerations effected on the Great Northern section of the East Coast route were made by good uphill running rather than so-called 'excessive' downhill running. Those who champion the Great Northern and its Stirling 8 ft 'singles', point to the fast starts and uphill workings, but the uphill work is no better than that performed by the 'Precedents' on the Crewe–Carlisle route or, indeed, that put in by the North British 4–4–0s north of Edinburgh. Aesthetically the Stirling 'singles' are a very pleasing design and it may be this factor which leads to their being very highly regarded locomotives, but, in strictly performance terms, they do not seem to be any more efficient than their counterparts on the other railways and may not even be as good as some – pretty looks apart.

The question of who started the races and when they became races might be said to stem from an initial decision by the East Coast to 'accelerate' the 8 p.m. ex-King's Cross from 1 July 1895. This particular 'acceleration' amounted to no more than a 15 minute reduction, though, as this announcement was made at the same time as one by the West Coast advertising a 10 minute reduction to the timings of its own 8 p.m. service, it can equally be interpreted as a relatively routine improvement in what was a less than exacting schedule, and one which was within the terms agreed after the races of 1888.

Two weeks later, on 14 July, the West Coast advertised that it would reduce the

*No. 775, this engine ran the Grantham–York section of the East Coast route on the last night of racing. The markings on the splasher, cabside and tender appear to be the work of the cleaners. (National Railway Museum)*

journey time of its 8 p.m. express to Aberdeen by 40 minutes, making the overall journey time 11 hours. The reduction was accompanied by an aggressive poster campaign. Huge blue posters were put up at Euston station and all the London & North Western's horse-drawn vehicles carried a similar message. This new West Coast acceleration cannot be regarded as routine in nature, a response was almost certainly called for and as events turned out, barely a week had gone by before the East Coast timetabled 'accelerations' to its own 8 p.m. Aberdeen express.

Prior to 14 July the 8 p.m. 'Scotch Express' was a well-loaded train, often of twenty carriages and usually hauled as far as Crewe by one of the three-cylinder 'Dreadnought' class compounds. At this time the booked average speeds for this journey were relatively slow even by 1890s standards: 48.3 m.p.h. between London and Bletchley, 47.8 m.p.h. between there and Rugby, and then rising again to 51.4 m.p.h. between Rugby and Crewe. Twenty coaches does seem rather a lot to be hauling, but at the time this would have resulted in a train weight in the region of 300 tons. The 'Dreadnought' compounds were one of the few locomotives of that era that could have handled 300 ton trains unassisted. From the introduction of the new schedules on 15 July, the loads were lightened and showed quite large variations, with a low of 110 tons on the nights of 19 July, 5 August and 11 August, to a high of 203 tons on the nights of 9 August and 16 August.

The run on 9 August was made by the 'Precedent' No. 394 *Eamont* as far as Rugby, where a stop was made for a pilot engine to be attached for the remainder of the journey through to Crewe. The running of the 16th was undertaken with one of the 'Dreadnought' compounds and was made unassisted throughout, taking 173 minutes to cover the 158.1 miles from Euston to Crewe, an average speed of 54.8 m.p.h. The reduced loadings and accelerated timings announced in July remained in operation until 19 August, when the load was again reduced – first to 95 tons and then, on the final night of the racing, to 72.5 tons.

The original 8 p.m. service called at Bletchley, Rugby, Crewe and Wigan en route to Carlisle. When the acceleration was announced these stops were cut out, and a relief train running behind the 8 p.m. carried goods, parcels and passengers to these places, the 8 p.m. being reserved for travellers to Aberdeen and Inverness. There were no departure times notified for stations en route and so the 8 p.m. 'Scotch Express' left each stop as soon as the locomotive had been changed or water taken.

The following week, on 22 July, the East Coast companies announced their own reduction and posted an arrival time in Aberdeen of 6.45 a.m. – a journey of 10 hours 45 minutes, or 15 minutes faster than the West Coast service. However, the West Coast was well prepared for any moves by its East Coast rivals and responded instantly by effecting another cut in its own schedule making the arrival time 6.35 a.m., 10 minutes earlier than the opposition. The West Coast's changed arrival time was not indicated in the public timetable though it does seem that travellers were aware that this was the case.

> The West Coast did not advertise the 6.35am arrival. It was, however, so well known in Scottish railway circles that it was evidently as good as advertised!
>
> Nock, *Railway Race to the North*, p. 78

From this point on there is no ambiguity whatsoever in the proceedings, whether they be called accelerations, re-timings, or improved schedules, racing was what was going on and is admitted as such in internal communications if not directly to the press and public:

> On the first day the East Coast were due in Aberdeen at 6.45am, the West Coast arrived at 6.39am. Whatever pretences might still be kept in England, there were no doubts in Scotland. It was another race, and with the two routes converging at Kinnaber Junction, a race of the most exciting kind. Aberdeen was agog. The running of the North British and Caledonian trains was a topic of conversation in all walks of life, and partisan feelings began to run high.
>
> Nock, *Railway Race to the North*, p. 78

On the ground, after 14 July the West Coast team had been using the booked 7.00 a.m. arrival time as little more than a guide, and had in fact arrived in Aberdeen as early as 6.21 a.m. and up until the 21st not later than 6.55 a.m., or 5 minutes early. The dating of the races is usually taken to be 22 July to 23 August, but the previous actions of the West Coast companies, running into Aberdeen as early as possible, could be interpreted as racing, in which case the start date would be 15 July. With arrivals of 20 and 40 minutes early during this week the West Coast was certainly making tremendous efforts to arrive first in Aberdeen, even if this does not actually constitute racing.

The night of 22/23 July, which was to have been the East Coast's 'winning' response to the West Coast's 7.00 a.m. arrival time, proved in the event to be rather a disappointing affair. Instead of arriving 15 minutes earlier than its rivals the East Coast was confronted with a re-timed West Coast service which had arrived in Aberdeen at 6.39 a.m. If this was round one the points must go to the West Coast.

The starting line-up of locomotives on that July night was, at King's Cross, engine No. 545 (a Stirling 8 ft 'single'), and for the opposition up the road at Euston, engine No. 394 *Eamont*. No. 545 had a train weighing approximately 179 tons and No. 394 *Eamont* had one of 140 tons. Several commentators and correspondents to the newspapers mentioned the issue of numbers of vehicles in the train and the weights of the trains, claiming that the West Coast ran lighter trains and thereby gained its winning advantage. The flaw in this argument is that if one compares the performances on a train weight to locomotive weight basis the figures are slightly different.

The two lightest racing loads, the 101 ton train on the East Coast on the night of 21/22 August and the 72.5 tons of the West Coast on the night of 22/23 August, give the following train-weight to engine-weight ratios:

| | | |
|---|---|---|
| Stirling 'single' | Nos 668 & 775 | 2.98 per cent |
| Webb 'Precedent' | No. 790 *Hardwicke* | 2.98 per cent |
| Holmes 4–4–0 | No. 293 | 2.95 per cent* |
| Worsdell 'Railcrusher' | Nos 1620 & 1621 | 2.80 per cent |
| Drummond 4–4–0 | No. 90 | 2.48 per cent |
| Lambie 4–4–0 | No. 17 | 2.46 per cent |

* Load reduced to 85 tons from Edinburgh

All figures from 'Summary of best engine performance',
Nock, *Railway Race to the North*, p. 134

Using this ratio shows how little difference there really was between the two sides in relation to the loads taken. Curiously, comparisons with other exceptional performances, including other record performances, show the train-to-engine weight ratio at around the 3 per cent figure. The Great Western's 4–4–0 No. 3440 *City of Truro* on her 100 m.p.h. Exeter–Bristol dash was with a train-to-engine weight ratio of 3.34 per cent. No. 6201 *Princess Elizabeth*'s run from Glasgow to Euston in 1936 was with a train-to-engine weight ratio of 2.97 per cent. The run from Swindon to Paddington in 1932, made at an average speed of 81.6 m.p.h., by No. 5006 *Tregenna Castle*, was another at a ratio of 2.95 per cent. Along with the above figures, in his *Railway Race to the North*, Nock lists some fourteen runs of note and with one exception all the ratios fall between 2.8 per cent and 3.67 per cent.

Nock offers another very interesting comparison in his book *Speed Records on Britain's Railways*, with a run that took place during the First World War on 4 June 1916. A special run had to be made at very short notice to convey documents from the Cabinet to Lord Kitchener, who was en route to Russia. Kitchener's train had left London at 5.45 p.m. and the special was put out in pursuit at 6.56 p.m.

The reason for choosing this comparison is presumably because the run was made in the same manner as the race of 1895, with the utmost alacrity. This feature apart, the remaining points of comparison have to be guessed at. The train weight in 1916 was only 70 tons compared with the 101 tons of the race train; the locomotives used in 1895 were a 2–2–2 and a 4–2–0, both designed by Stirling and both saturated steam engines, the 1916 motive power was a superheated 4–4–0 and an Ivatt 4–4–2, both substantially heavier and more powerful than the engines of 1895. However, the difference in time between King's Cross and Doncaster was a mere 2 minutes. The interesting comparison must surely be that in twenty years only 2 minutes improvement could be made, and that with stronger and heavier engines hauling a lighter load.

Making comparisons between different runs, with different train weights, different motive power, and even different motivators, is not an easy matter, after all war is a very different motivator from the money and kudos of 1895, and a superheated 4–4–0 is a vastly different form of motive power from a 2–2–2 saturated steam engine. Choosing to include it in this work is to highlight not only how little improvement had taken place in twenty years, but also the level of achievement involved in raising average speeds by as much as 15 and 20 m.p.h. in the six-week racing period.

On that first night of 'head-to-head' racing the London & North Western/Caledonian train ran into Aberdeen at 6.39 a.m. and the following day the arrival time was even earlier, being 6.30 a.m. This was what prompted the telegram from Oakley to Conacher, discussed earlier, which brought the remarkable reply from Lord Tweeddale, to beat the West Coast 'at all costs'.

On 29 July the East Coast inaugurated yet another new timetable, this time arrival was to be 6.25 a.m. However, the East Coast was once more destined to be disappointed, for the West Coast train arrived at 6.06 a.m., some 17 minutes earlier than the East Coast train which arrived 2 minutes early at 6.23 a.m. Round two to the West Coast crews.

The increases in speed at this early stage were still with more or less regular loads; the average weight for the ten heaviest loads between 22 July and 15 August was 164 tons for the West Coast trains. Only in the final days of the racing were the loads cut down to 100 tons or less. If the arrival times are compared, between 29 July and 18 August the only 'first' arrival made by the East Coast route was that of 18 August, at 6.17 a.m., when the West Coast arrived at 6.23 a.m. The earliest West Coast arrival was at 5.59 a.m. on 30 July, and the latest at 6.23 a.m. on 18 August. The corresponding East Coast figures are earliest on 18 August at 6.17 a.m. and latest at 7.05 a.m. on 4 August.

The contrast between the two routes is very noticeable: the one day where the East Coast's effort got them in first was the day of the West Coast's one late arrival. Generally the East Coast's figures are later overall arrival times with a pretty large number of late arrivals, which combine to make grim reading for those who would champion the East Coast. Even Nock has to agree, though his choice of phrase does seem a shade grudging.

> It must be conceded that between July 29th and August 18th the West Coast made by far the better showing.
>
> Nock, *Railway Race to the North*, p. 81

This period of the struggle, from late July through to mid-August, was being conducted at the height of the holiday season, just as the races of 1888 were. Grouse shooting was a very popular pastime during the last decades of Victoria's reign, and traffic to Scotland for the 'Glorious Twelfth' would have been at its peak during this time – making the West Coast's timekeeping record appear even more impressive. It is very likely that the reason no further advertised accelerations were made between 29 July and 19 August was the sheer volume of traffic for the start of the grouse season.

Whatever the volume of traffic, the period between 29 July and 19 August cannot be described as a quiet one, and some excellent runs were made hauling not inconsiderable loads. Engine No. 749 *Mercury* ran from Euston to Crewe at an average speed of 55.8 m.p.h. with a load of 195 tons on 2 August. On 18 August the stalwart No. 790 *Hardwicke* took 188 tons over the same route at an average of 56.1 m.p.h. The Crewe–Carlisle road saw some of the most exciting of the running, for in addition to the efforts of No. 790 *Hardwicke* on the night of the record, the run by fireman Hughes and driver Rowe with engine No. 1213 *The Queen* took eleven coaches equal to 172 tons, unassisted, over the 141 miles in 159 minutes. Some idea of the effort in this run can be adjudged from the fact that at this time loads of over twelve coaches were assisted throughout.

The same crew and engine, but assisted by engine No. 622 *Prince Albert*, took 203 tons (a train of some thirteen coaches) through from Crewe to Carlisle in 152 minutes. The record-setting pair of driver Robinson and fireman Wolstencroft, with engine No. 1683 *Sisyphus*, attempted to take twelve coaches unassisted on the night of 18 August, but were ultimately forced to stop and take banking assistance from Tebay up to Shap summit. This stop caused such a delay that the arrival time in Carlisle was 1.49 a.m., the latest time since 21 July and this was, of course, the one night in the whole period when the East Coast were first to arrive in Aberdeen.

During the races the first faster than mile-a-minute timings over this section were accomplished by the Crewe–Carlisle team of driver Phillips and fireman Kay with engine No. 1683 *Sisyphus* on 19 August, when they made the trip in 140 minutes, though the load on this occasion was only 95 tons. (The first mile-a-minute time ever set on this journey was that of the 'Precedent' No. 275 *Vulcan* during the race of 1888. *Vulcan* ran the 90.1 miles from Preston to Carlisle in 90 minutes.) The next night, 20 August, the pairing of Robinson and Wolstencroft, with engine No. 790 *Hardwicke* and the same load, made the 141 mile run in 134 minutes; Phillips and Kay responded with a run of 135 minutes on the 21st. Between 15 July, when the arrival time at Carlisle was 1.48 a.m., journey times gradually decreased until, on the final night's racing, the arrival time at Carlisle was down to 12.36 a.m. – a reduction of almost 1 hour 15 minutes on the Euston–Carlisle journey time, achieved in less than six weeks of running.

No sooner had the grouse season started on 12 August than the East Coast companies met in York to hold a council of war. Present at this meeting were superintendent of the line, David Deuchars, and locomotive engineer, Matthew Holmes, for the North British. Vincent Raven, who held the post of locomotive running superintendent and was made assistant mechanical engineer to Wilson Worsdell in 1895, was attending on behalf of the North Eastern, as was John Welburn, the superintendent of the line. Cockshott sent his assistant J. Alexander to attend to matters for the Great Northern.

This meeting, which had been called to discuss what action to take in regard to the continued challenge of the West Coast companies, decided that from 19 August to the 23rd the arrival time in Aberdeen should be made 5.40 a.m. Another of those odd little inconsistencies pops up here. Nock states,

> Up till then the earliest Caledonian arrival in Aberdeen had been 6.06a.m.
>
> Nock, *Railway Race to the North*, p. 90

However, a table of arrival times on page 129 of Nock's *Railway Race to the North* shows that on 30 July the West Coast train arrived in Aberdeen at 5.59 a.m. The reason for this discrepancy is not clear.

The minutes of the meeting, from which Nock quotes, show that the East Coast train should not have exceeded seven coaches and should have, where possible, run with no more than six. It was also agreed that no passengers destined for south of Dundee would be carried, thus putting the service on the same basis as that employed by the West Coast. There is also another remark which seems to indicate that Mr Alexander, for the Great Northern, was unsure as to how much faster the Great Northern could run.

> The foregoing times are subject to alteration if the Great Northern Company can to-morrow [*sic*] see their way to further acceleration.
>
> Minutes of meeting of senior East Coast officers at York, held on
> 13 August 1895, from Nock, *Railway Race to the North*, p. 90

The York meeting produced a flurry of correspondence between the principal operating officers of the Great Northern. On 14 August Patrick Stirling wrote to his district superintendent in Peterborough, a Mr Rouse, urging him to put his men 'on their mettle!' Two days later, on 16 August, Rouse was sent another letter, headed 'Race to Aberdeen'; the letter contains a quite remarkable instruction:

> The drivers must not study economy of fuel in the race, but must beat the North Western, whatever they may burn in the way of fuel of the best selected quality.
>   Tell them please that this will be fully allowed for in the distribution of premiums, and further, Mr. Stirling thinks it will be well to give the men some extra pecuniary allowance, such as a ¼ day's pay whenever they arrive on time, or in any other way by douceur or otherwise that may best secure the end in view.
>
> Nock, *Railway Race to the North*, p. 94

Despite the urgings of Stirling and the proffered inducements, the point-to-point average speeds scheduled by the Great Northern were slower than those set by the North Eastern. On the final night of the racing by the East Coast, the scheduled time from King's Cross to Grantham was 109 minutes and the actual time taken was 101 minutes, a saving of 8 minutes in a distance of 105 miles. The booked average speed for the King's Cross to Grantham run is less than a mile a minute; the North Eastern on the other hand was timed to run the 80.6 miles from York to Newcastle in 80 minutes and only 129 minutes were scheduled for the 124.4 miles from Newcastle to Edinburgh. On the last night the time over the Newcastle–Edinburgh section was cut to 113 minutes, which represents double the amount of time gained between London and Grantham by the Great Northern.

During the week 12–18 August the West Coast had arrived in Aberdeen at 6.12 a.m., 6.15 a.m., 6.13 a.m., 6.18 a.m., 6.10 a.m., and on the 18th at 6.23 a.m. On 19 August, the day so carefully planned by the East Coast to scupper the efforts of their rivals, the West Coast train arrived in Aberdeen at 5.15 a.m., 25 minutes ahead of the East Coast's booked time of arrival of 5.40 a.m. The performance was no 'flash in the pan', for it was repeated on the 20th when the West Coast ran in at 4.58 a.m., 13 minutes ahead of the East Coast, though at the crucial point of Kinnaber Junction the gap was only 1 minute.

> The Caledonian was first, if by no more than a minute, and passed Kinnaber Junction at 4.22a.m. The North British, slacking through Montrose, and then pounding up the heavy grade to Hillside, passed through at 4.26a.m. At the most critical points of all, Dubton on the one hand and Montrose on the other, the passing times were 4.21a.m and 4.22a.m. respectively.
>
> Nock, *Railway Race to the North*, p. 110

This has to be round three to the West Coast, for not only did they beat off the secretly planned challenge of the 19th, they also ran in first on the 20th, setting more than a mile-a-minute time for the whole journey including stops, and this when the East Coast was posting its best time to date by arriving at 5.11 a.m.

*A North British 4–4–0 heads a rake of mostly six-wheel coaches over the Caledonian's metals into Aberdeen. While this is not the race train itself it is a very typical train of the 1890s era. (National Railway Museum)*

On the night of 21/22 August the East Coast companies did succeed in arriving first, running in at a new record time of 4.40 a.m. and having done so they called a halt to their racing. Nock comments,

> When at last the East Coast companies had cast off the lingering shackles of orthodox railway operating they won a great victory, but instead of staying to consolidate the advantage of their shorter route they cried 'Pax' and quit the field.

Nock, *Railway Race to the North*, p. 129

It is curious that the decision of the meeting was to run the accelerated time until the 23rd; in the event they called a halt on the 22nd. The 'great victory', or at least arriving first on this one occasion seems to have been taken as all the proof necessary to proclaim that the East Coast companies were 'winners'. When compared with the performances of the West Coast team it is difficult to see the East Coast claim as much more than a one-off. Having managed to get into Aberdeen first in this particular instance, the East Coast management appear to be only too pleased to be able to call it all off,

> Fear of disaster was chief motivator for Conacher deciding on the arrival of the train at Aberdeen on the final night that enough was enough and the nonsense must end.
>
> Thomas, The North British Railway, p. 53

The following day, 23 August, when the West Coast re-took the record, Conacher changed his mind and wanted to have another go and actually persuaded Stegman Gibb on the North Eastern to join in. However, Oakley refused, which seems an odd decision when it was he who took most persuading to halt the racing after the arrival at 4.40 a.m. on the 22nd. The answer seems to lie in a series of telegrams (reproduced in Nock, *Railway Race to the North*) which were exchanged between Conacher, Gibb and Oakley:

> After this morning's achievement I think we ought tonight to revert to advertised time, making another effort later on if the West Coast do better. There is a feeling here that rivalry has gone far enough already and I think we might rest on the position gained unless again challenged when we can choose our own time for another effort. Have wired Gibb also. Shall be here all day.
>
> Conacher (p. 115)

> I think we ought to continue to shew [*sic*] our friends the hopelessness of their effort. Stopping now would be commented on. Please reply.
>
> Oakley (p. 116)

> Having made record this morning my opinion in favour of confining racing to this week. Best policy to be able to prove that except this week we have worked our trains not as racers but under ordinary traffic conditions.
>
> Gibb (p. 116)

> There are so many chances against our repeating last night's performance tonight and tomorrow night, especially as everything depends on reaching Kinnaber first, that I hesitate to risk spoiling it. If however you think otherwise I agree, but if you can do even better it ought to be done as West Coast will be sure to make great efforts tonight.
>
> Conacher (p. 116)

Gibb suggests we continue this week. Have told you propose ceasing tonight. Feeling of directors here that we should cease having shewn [*sic*] what we can do. Reply now.

Oakley (p. 116)

Your second telegram received. Am glad your directors agree to view expressed in my first telegram. I think it the safest course and most dignified. Wire here whether it is the 6.25 arrival going back to and I will instruct our people. Details can be settled by Superintendents.

Conacher (p. 117)

The only conclusion to be arrived at is that there was a great deal of nervousness and indecision, not quite the qualities of leadership one expects from a forthright and fearless management under instruction to 'stop at nothing', 'beat them at all costs', and be 'determined to beat them at their own game', as various parties stated at one time or another. However, the fact that lives could be put at risk was ever present and though this did not seem to worry the management when it was only employees who were dying, the possibility that members of the public might be involved made matters a little different. In addition, as the accelerations were all of the management's own doing, it would be their heads on the block if trouble did occur, a consideration which does appear to have had a sobering effect on those 'great railwaymen'.

There also appears to be more than a little self-delusion in the exchange of letters which follow the telegraphic communications:

I am not much concerned by the empty honour won by the North Western as the fact of their reducing the weight of their train is a practical confession that on equal terms they would be unable to compete with us.

Our view is strongly that we should continue our present times of running so as to put steady pressure on the West Coast which they can only sustain at increased cost and for very poor results, while we can practically run an ordinary train, and carry the bulk of the people.

Oakley (p. 125)

The difference in train weights and numbers of coaches has already been discussed, the only other comment to make here is that the train run by the West Coast on the final night had almost as much passenger accommodation as that of the East Coast and, in general terms, the loadings throughout the races had been broadly comparable and, as such, do little to justify Sir Henry's bold claims and references to an 'empty honour'.

Whether it is right to claim the East Coast had 'won a great victory' is a moot point really; after all, the 'lingering shackles of orthodox railway operating' were cast off on 19 and 20 August, and in the wee small hours of the 23rd the West Coast regained the record. Rhetorically Nock asks, 'Who won?' He goes on to say that 'The question does not admit of a definite answer.' However, if one begins to consider some of the measures one could employ in trying to determine 'who won' – reliability, punctuality, best overall time and highest overall average – and then look at which route takes the honours in these categories, it is hard not to consider the claim of the West Coast route.

Over the six weeks of racing, between them, the five companies involved used a number of different types of locomotives. The most modern were the 4–4–0s used by the Caledonian, North British and North Eastern companies. The oldest of the designs were those of Patrick Stirling, the 2–2–2s and the 4–2–0 8 ft 1 in 'singles', which were first introduced in 1870. These Great Northern locomotive designs were closely followed in age if not beauty by the London & North Western's 'Precedent' 2–4–0s, and sandwiched in between these and the more modern 4–4–0s were the London & North Western's 'Dreadnought' class compounds. Newest of all were the Lambie 4–4–0s, first appearing in 1894 as a variant of the Drummond 4–4–0, which in turn had first been used by the Caledonian in 1882 after Drummond's defection from the North British. The Lambie 4–4–0 was used by driver John Soutar over the Perth–Aberdeen section. The Holmes's 4–4–0s, which were used on the North British, were introduced in 1891, and like the Lambie 4–4–0s, these engines too were based on an original design of Drummond and first came into operation in 1876.

The Worsdell 'M' class which first entered traffic in 1892 shouldered most of the burden on the North Eastern, but by no means all of it. The 'Ms' of Wilson Worsdell were supported by the class 'Js' introduced by Worsdell's elder brother who was chief mechanical engineer to the North Eastern prior to Wilson Worsdell's appointment. T.W. Worsdell designed the 'J' class as compound engines, though at the time of the races many had been converted to simple engines by his brother, Wilson. The performances these engines gave over the York to Newcastle section were only marginally slower than those of the 'Ms', and on other occasions they were used as pilot engines in tandem with the 'M' class on the Newcastle–Edinburgh run.

The surprising feature of the locomotive comparisons is that the tiny 33 ton 'Precedents' performed at least as well as their much newer and heavier sisters, the 50 ton 4–4–0 Worsdell 'M' class, the first of which rolled out of the workshops in December of 1892. The 'M' class, as originally designed, had cylinders of 19 in by 26 in, the heating surface was 1,341 sq ft, the grate area was 19.5 sq ft and the driving wheels were 7 ft 1 in. The 'Precedents', by comparison, had cylinders of 17 in by 24 in, a heating surface of 1,102 sq ft and a grate area of 17.1 sq ft, with 6 ft 9 in driving wheels. The essential feature and, indeed, the secret of the success of these little engines, was the efficiency of the design of the valves and steam ports in reducing back pressure in the cylinders. Given the degree of conflicting evidence about the work of their designer, Francis William Webb, whether this design was arrived at via well-tried principles or purely by chance will doubtless remain one of life's little mysteries.

The 4–4–0s used by the Caledonian and North British were all remarkably similar in proportion, indeed the Lambie 4–4–0 used by John Soutar on the Perth–Aberdeen stretch was a straightforward development of the Drummond-designed engines used by Crooks and Robinson on the Carlisle–Perth runs. The Holmes 4–4–0s of the North British were also developments of the same general

*Throughout the races the North British 4–4–0s certainly put in their fair share of effort in attempting to do down their opposite numbers on the Caledonian. The cabs of these Holmes adapations of Drummond's original design are very reminiscent of those of Stirling's engines for the Great Northern, while the dome-mounted safety valves are very much Drummond's handiwork. (National Railway Museum)*

family of Drummond 4–4–0s, the '476' class of 1876. These engines had 18 in by 26 in cylinders, a total heating surface of 1,099.3 sq ft, a 21 sq ft grate area and 6 ft 6 in driving wheels. The leading dimensions of both Holmes's and Lambie's engines were practically identical; on the Lambie engines the boiler pressure had been increased from 150 p.s.i. to 160 p.s.i. and the dome-mounted safety valves used by Drummond were replaced by a set fitted over the firebox crown. The Lambie engines had cylinders of 18 in by 26 in, a heating surface of 1,184 sq ft, a grate area of 19.5 sq ft, and 6 ft 6 in driving wheels. The Holmes '633' class, by comparison, had 18 in by 26 in cylinders, 1,266 sq ft of heating surface, a grate area of 21 sq ft, 6 ft 6 in drivers and a boiler pressure of 150 p.s.i.

The influence of both Peter and Dougal Drummond on Scottish locomotive design and practice was enormous when one considers that between them they provided locomotives and designs for both goods and passenger traffic for no less than four of Scotland's major railway companies between 1875 and 1918: North British, Caledonian, Glasgow & South Western, and the Highland Railways. Another example to add to the Worsdells and Drummonds, in the brothers-in-office theme, is that of Patrick and James Stirling who held office on the Glasgow & South Western between 1853 and 1878. Patrick went to the Great Northern in

1866 and James took over the reins at the Glasgow & South Western following Patrick's departure.

The use of compounding in British locomotive practice is a veritable minefield of conflicting information, opinion and performance. In the races only the London & North Western used a compound-type locomotive – the 'Dreadnought' class engine – with No. 1301 *Teutonic* on the run of 21 July, No. 1307 *Coptic* hauling the race train on 16 August and No. 1309 *Adriatic*, which made the Euston–Crewe run on the last four race days, 19-22 August. On the very last night of the racing, No. 1309 *Adriatic* averaged 64.2 m.p.h. between Euston and Crewe. Despite their use in the races these engines have been described as:

> A powerful, but not altogether reliable engine – troublesome in starting and sluggish at express speed.
>
> Nock, *Railway Enthusiast's Encyclopedia*, p. 112

Adverse comments notwithstanding, these engines did not prove unreliable in the races, and it was one of their number that was chosen to make the first non-stop run between Euston and Carlisle, not the type of task one would readily allot to an unreliable locomotive. It does seem highly unlikely that Webb, who designed them, would have remained chief locomotive engineer to the world's largest company for over twenty years if the locomotives he built were unreliable. Despite being labelled sluggish and unreliable, there is the admission that at the time of the races these engines were one of the few types then in service capable of hauling 300 ton trains unassisted. The 'Dreadnoughts' had two outside high-pressure cylinders measuring 14 in by 24 in and one inside low-pressure cylinder 30 in by 24 in. The heating surface was 1,361 sq ft and the grate area was 20.5 sq ft. The driving wheels, which were uncoupled, were 6 ft 3 in in diameter and the engines weighed 42.5 tons; only the 'Precedents' and the Stirling 2–2–2s were lighter and this latter type was only 2.75 tons less.

The overall performances by both crews and locomotives in relation to highest speeds and best averages stand up well to subsequent performances. However, the record of consistency shown by the West Coast route is the real achievement of this competition. The high speeds and point-to-point averages were all beaten over the following forty years, but the record time of 512 minutes for the 540 miles is still a record today for steam locomotive traction.

*Chapter Six*

# AFTER THE BALL WAS OVER

Following the ending of the races both routes reverted to rather less demanding schedules, which was only to be expected. The difficulty was that the races had made no alterations in the business problems that the management had to resolve; labour problems like those of 1891 intensified, leading to a national rail strike in 1911. The sixteen years between 1895 and 1911 saw the railwayman's average earnings rise from 24s per week to 25s 9d, and the sixty-hour week was still a commonplace. The appalling state of the relations between the unions and the railway companies can be gauged from the fact that the government was forced to intervene in the 1911 strike in a manner it may well have preferred not to, ordering the management to meet with the union representatives. Murphy and Field, in their work on the centenary of the locomens' union Aslef, commented:

> The railway companies could refuse to recognise the Trade Unions. They
> could hardly refuse to recognise the House of Commons.
> Murphy & Field, ASLEF 1880–1980, p. 25

No sooner had the railways returned to something approaching normality following the national strike, than the outbreak of the First World War saw them put under State control through the use of the 1871 Regulation of Forces Act. The actual hands-on control was the responsibility of the Railway Executive Committee, which was mainly comprised of the general managers of the country's leading railway companies. On the face of it nothing had changed: the railway was still under the control of the same men, dividends would be paid, and rank and file railwaymen could be made to 'tighten their belts' to do their bit for the war effort. Things had changed though; the ordinary passenger and businessman no longer came first and foremost, now it was the needs of the State in managing the war effort; nor were general managers having to produce an operating profit, the government having guaranteed dividends at 1913 levels. Though this period was not quite the death knell for railway independence, it did further the continuing process of amalgamation.

The process of growth through amalgamation, so much a feature of the landscape of earlier railway expansion, still had a little way to run when the East Coast quit racing in August 1895. After the ending of hostilities in 1918 the two largest of all the amalgamations took place: first, the London & North Western and Lancashire & Yorkshire became one company in 1921. There were one or two unusual aspects to this particular amalgamation, which had initially been proposed in the 1870s and for some time the two companies had been operating a traffic pooling agreement for the distribution of the profits over certain of their routes. The Lancashire & Yorkshire was a profitable concern with a good record of dividends, though of course much smaller in size than the London & North Western, yet despite the difference in size the Lancashire & Yorkshire officers took the senior posts, Arthur Watson being made general manager and George Hughes becoming chief mechanical engineer in the newly expanded company.

Large as this amalgamation was, it was but a curtain-raiser for what was to follow in 1923, when the second amalgamation took place. One hundred and twenty-three railway companies – practically every railway in the country – became the 'Big Four' in the grandest amalgamation of them all, most commonly referred to as the Grouping. In addition to the continuing growth by amalgamation in the post-race era, the railway network itself was still physically expanding. Sir Edward Watkin's Manchester, Sheffield & Lincoln changed its name and became the Great Central Railway in 1897. Under its new name, the Great Central opened its own route into central London in 1899, with a new terminus at Marylebone.

The synchronicities which have popped up at various points in railway affairs over the years put in another appearance in the Great Central's London extension saga. The decision to build the London extension was heavily criticized and shareholders did not receive any dividends from it, not that there was anything particularly unusual in this, as many other lines did not pay either. What was both sad and short-sighted about the Great Central's London extension was that it was one of the first main line routes to be axed in the Beeching era, and yet it was the only main line route out of central London to the North which was built to the Continental loading gauge, thus making it the ideal route for traffic north from the Channel Tunnel. During the period when the Channel Tunnel was under construction the Canadian Pacific shipping and transport group spent a million pounds on a feasibility study to see if this route could be re-opened and used for its traffic. This is perhaps even more ironic when one remembers that Sir Edward Watkin received his knighthood for his work on the Grand Trunk Railway of Canada, Canadian Pacific's rival, and was involved in an abortive scheme to put a tunnel under the Channel in Victoria's reign.

Never a group to be left out of the growth and continued development of the railways, the locomotive engineers were still producing new innovations in the early decades of the twentieth century, the most significant of which was the introduction of 'superheating' in 1906.

Superheating, the invention of which dates from 1898 and is credited to the German locomotive engineer Schmidt, is a process for applying additional heat to the saturated steam produced in the normal way in the boiler. The saturated steam is not passed directly to the cylinders but is first passed through a series of tubes which are heated by the very hot gases coming off the fire. This has the effect of evaporating more of the water droplets suspended in the saturated steam thus increasing its volume and hence the amount of work it is capable of producing. Overall, the effect is a saving in coal consumption which in some cases could be as much as 25 per cent.

Along with the superheater, the injector – the most commonly used form of valve gear on outside cylinder locomotives built after the First World War – and the major developments in blastpipe design, were all as a result of the work of foreign engineers: Walschearts, Giffard, Chapeleon, Kyalami and Giesel. The first purpose-built locomotive test bed was, likewise, a Continental creation.

Despite the existence of looming problems in numerous areas of their businesses, the desire to race shown by some elements within the railway management structure, did not disappear after 1895, it merely changed its *modus operandi*. Testing, scientific or otherwise, became a new area in which high-speed running could be legitimized; after all, no one could complain if experiments were being carried out to determine the most efficient and cost effective designs or safest types of equipment. There is another factor at play, that of 'public image'. The races of 1888, and more so in 1895, had shown the companies the extent of public interest in the spectacle, the 'glamour' of high-speed trains and the possibilities inherent in long distance, non-stop, high-speed services to major cities. The altered nature of the services the railways were introducing was, of course, another means to continue the experimentation: to design newer and more powerful locomotives to haul greater loads over longer distances at higher overall average speeds and, at the same time, deliver lowered operating costs. At least, that was the theory.

If the races could be said to have a legacy then it must surely be in raising the levels not only of speeds, but also of the numbers of regular scheduled services operating at high overall averages. By the outbreak of the Second World War over 170 services had point-to-point averages of over a mile a minute and more than 200 others were running at averages between 58 and 60 m.p.h. Though some of these averages were over distances of only 20 or 30 miles some of them were for distances of as much as 268 miles on the East Coast between London and Newcastle. Indeed, on this route, the whole 392.5 mile journey between London and Edinburgh could be undertaken faster than a mile a minute. The West Coast's timings were lower than those on the East, but nevertheless, it had services which covered the 299 miles between London and Carlisle in 283 minutes. After the ending of the Second World War it was not until the 1960s that services returned to these pre-war levels and they did so only when new forms of traction took over.

There are other changes at the beginning of the twentieth century and in the immediate post-Grouping period which can be described as being extensions of the 'racing trains syndrome'. The alterations taking place in locomotive size, design and construction in the post-race age can be divided into several categories: new production techniques, new materials, scientific testing and new sources of power (electricity and diesel oil). Some steam locomotives were even converted to oil burners, though this was a short-lived experiment in Britain.

New production methods incorporated changes such as moves away from riveting to new techniques of welding, the availability of new types of machine tools and the increasing use of electricity to light and drive workshops, though these changes cannot be said to have produced any high degree of innovation in locomotive design. The *Rocket* may not have had injectors, superheating or a self-

*One of Worsdell's 'Q' class 4–4–0s specially adapted for conducting trials on, among other things, the smokebox vacuum. The strange-looking box mounted alongside the smokebox allowed an employee to sit inside while the locomotive was in motion and watch what was happening in the smokebox through a window cut into the side of the smokebox. As the twentieth century wore on more sophisticated methods of testing replaced the crude earlier attempts. (National Railway Museum)*

cleaning smokebox, but it did have outside cylinders, a multi-tube boiler and a smokebox vacuum. The men who built the engines which ran in the Rainhill Trials in 1829 would have had little difficulty in recognizing Britain's last steam locomotive, the 2–10–0 '9F' named *Evening Star*, as she rolled out of Swindon Works in 1962.

In the first decade of the twentieth century, locomotive exchange trials began to pop up all over the place including in the United States, though there had been exchange trials prior to 1900. In 1870 the London & South Western and South Eastern Railways held exchange trials to help determine firebox designs and in 1898 the Lancashire & Yorkshire swopped with the Great Northern, an exchange which seems to have been an 'old pals' type of event – Ivatt on the Great Northern and Aspinall on the Lancashire & Yorkshire had both worked for Irish Railways. In the twentieth century though, the trials became bigger, longer and more widespread. In 1907 the North British and North Eastern began a series of exchanges which ran until 1911, in 1908 the North Eastern was swopping compounds with the Midland, and in 1909 the London & North Western was looking to improve its locomotive stock and, particularly, the 'Experiment' and 'Precursor' classes of George Whale.

C.J. Bowen-Cooke had taken over as chief mechanical engineer from Whale in March 1909 and he organized to borrow one of the 'Cardean' Class 4–6–0s from the Caledonian, one of Earle Marsh's superheated 4–4–2 tank engines, No. 23, and one of the Great Northern's Ivatt Atlantics, engine No. 1449. The London & North Western sent engine No. 510 *Albatross* to compete against the Great Northern's Atlantic No. 1451, while on its own metals engine No. 412 *Marquis* flew the flag. The results, declared in terms of pounds-per-mile coal consumption, were more or less a dead heat: the Ivatt Atlantic returned figures of 41.08 lb per mile and the 'Precursor' 40.73 lb per mile. 'Precursor' class No. 7 *Titan* went over to the London, Brighton & South Coast in exchange for the 4–4–2T No. 23. No. 23, being the only superheated engine in the exchanges, duly showed the rest a clean pair of heels with figures of 27 lb per mile coal consumption and 22 gallons per mile of water evaporated.

The trials using the Caledonian 'Cardean' class 4–6–0s and the London & North Western's 4–6–0 'Experiment' class involved a locomotive destined to be written off in 1915 after being involved in one of the worst railway accidents of all time, that at Quintinshill a few miles outside of Gretna to the north of Carlisle. The engine 'Cardean' class No. 907 was destroyed beyond economic repair in this disaster, which claimed more than 225 lives and left another 245 seriously injured. In the trials No. 907 was paired against No. 1405 *City of Manchester*, while engine No. 903 *Cardean* was matched with No. 2630 *Buffalo*. The coal consumption of these 4–6–0s was considerably higher than those for the 4–4–0s and the 4–4–2s, being in the region of 70 to 80 lb per mile, or almost double that of the smaller engines.

The following year, 1910, there was another exchange, this time involving the Great Western, with the London & North Western utilizing one of the Great Western's 'Star' class engines No. 4005 *Polar Star*, while the Great Western had the use of one of the London & North Western's 'Experiment' class engines, No. 1471 *Worcestershire*. Though these exchanges cannot really be described as racing, they were definitely contests, in that every effort was made to discover the fullest extent of the locomotive's capabilities, just as they were in dynamometer car trials conducted on the 'Claughton' class engine No. 1159 *Ralph Brocklebank*, only months before the First World War broke out. Locomotive tests and exchanges such as these took place at various times right through and into the nationalization era.

On the Northern Division main line the 'George the Fifths' and the 'Prince of Wales' 4–6–0s quickly replaced the non-superheated 'Experiments', but it was the work of the 'Claughton' that attracted the greatest attention. For a time the pioneer engine of the class was regularly allotted to the 5.19p.m. West Coast Corridor from Crewe to Carlisle, and achieved a fine reputation for punctual working, while the dynamometer car test on the 10a.m. ex-

Euston, on November 4th, 1913 with engine No. 1159 *Ralph Brocklebank* is one of the classics of British locomotive performance.

Nock, *North Western*, p. 272

In America, between 1900 and 1905, there were tests and trials conducted over the routes between New York and Chicago. These events brought the journey time between the two cities down from 28 hours to 18 hours. In this particular competition there was an important signpost to future trends. The New York Central Railroad was deemed to have come out on top, not because of any superior running or technology, but because it employed the better sales and marketing techniques.

There was another important development at this time which the railways failed to come to terms with, for it was in this period that the road lobby began to establish itself. One of the major failings of railway management was the inability to register the degree to which the growth of road transport would undermine its core business. The slowness of the railway companies to react to the impact of the family saloon car and the perceived benefits of road freight and the 'too little too late' means used to combat this threat, have had the most disastrous consequences for the taxpayer and the environment. Even quality of life can be said to have been blighted by the ever-increasing use of road transport, the growth of which is the mirror image of the railway's decline.

The late A.J.P. Taylor argued, convincingly, that the First World War was fought to the German Railway Timetable, or at least to the one put in place for the planned mobilization. During these hostilities, there were tests and trials to determine what would be the best type of goods engine for use by the Railway Operating Department. This was the operational side of the railways equivalent to the Railway Executive Committee and involved the leading engineers from a variety of the country's leading railway companies. The design eventually chosen was a 2–8–0 based on the work of the Great Central Railway's chief mechanical engineer, J.G. Robinson. For many years after the war, until withdrawn from traffic, these engines and some very similar ones built by the Great Western were known by the acronym RODS.

After the war and the Grouping of 1923, there followed the British Empire Exhibition held at Wembley in 1924. At this exhibition, where Nigel Gresley's engine No. 4472 *Flying Scotsman* was displayed adjacent to C.B. Collett's locomotive No. 4073 *Caerphilly Castle*, there was a good deal of speculation as to the merits and capabilities of the two engines. The outcome of these speculations was that arrangements were put in hand to hold a full series of comparative tests to take place in late April and early May 1925.

The London & North Eastern sent engine No. 4474 *Victor Wild*, manned by driver Pibworth and fireman Birkwood, over to the Great Western where it competed against engine No. 4074 *Caldicot Castle*, crewed by driver Rowe and fireman Cook. In exchange the Great Western despatched No. 4079 *Pendennis Castle*, with driver William Young in control, to the London & North Eastern where it ran against engine No. 2545 *Diamond Jubilee*. Despite being both heavier, longer and of a more powerful appearance than the 'Castle' class engines Gresley's

*The scene could almost be the locomotive exchanges of 1925 or even those of 1948 as the 'Castle' class locomotives were featured in both, though the 'The Cornishman' headboard would seem a little out of place. Here No. 5029* Nunney Castle *is accelerating away from Loughborough on the former Great Central Railway main line, now preserved by the Mainline Steam Trust.*

'A1', later 'A3', Pacifics were comprehensively beaten, the 'Castles' returning better coal consumption figures and maintaining higher overall average speeds. To Gresley's credit, it must be said that he modified his engines following the exchanges, increasing both valve lap and valve travel, bringing his design closer to that of Collett's and improving all round the performance of the 'A3s' in the process.

Like the races of 1895, these events were brought to the attention of the public and as in 1895 the public saw them for what they were:

> By the public it was regarded as a sporting event of the first magnitude, and the interest on all hands was enormous.
>
> Allen, *The Locomotive Exchanges*, p. 38

These trials were followed, in 1926, by a similar one on the London, Midland & Scottish Railway; again the Great Western loaned out one of its 'Castle' class engines. The interesting comparison in this particular exchange was that the best of the 'Castle' class runs took 157 minutes over the 141 miles from Crewe to Carlisle, which No. 790 *Hardwicke* had run in 126 minutes in 1895!

If there can be said to have been a spin-off from the trials on the London & North Eastern, it must surely have been the inauguration of the non-stop service from London to Edinburgh in 1928, which, in turn, can be seen as the forerunner of the streamlined services introduced in September 1935 and named 'Silver Jubilee', in honour of George V's twenty-five years on the throne. Before public services commenced on these new streamlined high-speed services, attempts to create new 'top speed' records were made by both the London, Midland & Scottish Railway and the London & North Eastern Railway, which were the new names for the amalgamations of the old companies which had originally formed the East Coast and West Coast routes. These events have been given the status of 'braking trials', ironic in view of the repeated criticism of the Great Northern and its brakes by the Railway Inspectorate. The 'braking trials' were supposedly to determine the stopping distances at a variety of speeds and under varying load conditions. However, for many, and for Nigel Gresley in particular, the real nature of these events was to see how fast it was possible to make the locomotives travel, rather than how long it took to stop them. After all, management could not possibly condone flat-out speed record attempts any more than they could admit to racing.

> Though he successfully exploited the very real advantages of fast uphill running in the attainment of fast average speeds, Gresley had never lost his enthusiasm for high speed. . . . He had consistently encouraged bursts of high speed in the various preludes to the faster trains, and Silver Fox had attained 113mph in August 1936: but, since 29th June 1937, the British record of 114mph rested with Stanier's Pacific. The World Record of 124.4mph had been set by a German 4–6–4 in June 1936.
>
> Bulleid, *Master Builders of Steam*, p. 69

Continuing his resume of Gresley's work for the LNER, Bulleid describes the events leading up to *Mallard*'s record run:

> The opportunity [to beat the LMS and the German records] would present itself during the brake trials he was continually arranging, which were aimed at reducing the time taken for a full application of the vacuum brake on the engine to be effective at the rear of the train. This took about 10 seconds on a train 674ft. long weighing 333 tons, but had been reduced to 3 seconds with a Westinghouse Quick Service valve. . . . Gresley fitted the Quick Service valves to the high speed trains in 1938 and started another series of brake tests. For those tests on 3rd July 1938, class 'A4' Pacific No. 4468, *Mallard* was chosen. She was only a few weeks old, her free-running capabilities had the help of the Kylchap double blast pipe [designed by Chapeleon and Kyalami] and chimney – and besides Gresley had an affection for the common wild duck. Newsome was as usual in charge of the tests and driver Duddington was on the engine. Gresley rode in the ex-N.E.R dynamometer car; the train weight was 240 tons gross.
>
> Bulleid, *Master Builders of Steam*, p. 69

*The man and his engine. Sir Nigel Gresley with one of his 'A4' Pacifics, which had been named in his honour. Why the shed yard was chosen as the setting for the photograph is not clear. (National Railway Museum)*

The races, and the various trials and tests which came after them, led to new and more sophisticated means of measuring locomotive performance being adopted. These newer and more scientific means of testing led to improvements in valve and steam port design, new blast-pipe designs and led to increased fuel economy and boiler efficiency. The quest to improve locomotive design and efficiency led the French to build a static test centre at Vitry-sur-Seine, which opened in September 1933. Nigel Gresley attended the opening and was one of the first British locomotive engineers to send his locomotives to the centre for testing, though there is scant evidence that he used the results from the test in any systematic way.

Increasing the scientific content of locomotive testing led to improvements and innovations which undoubtedly did improve the efficiency of the locomotive, but these improvements can really only be described as minor. They saved on materials and construction costs, they helped to keep axle weights down and made life marginally easier for the footplatemen, but the overall design was unaltered. The real problems were not those of the difference in efficiency between one locomotive type or another, or even over valve design and air flow through the fire bed, they were those of different types of investment and more efficient forms of traction, and no amount of scientific testing of steam locomotion would alter these parameters.

The use of steam to power railways, and other forms of transport, continued to decline as the twentieth century progressed. One of the more important factors in this decline, leaving aside the improvements to, and expanded use of, the diesel and internal combustion engine, was because there was a general failure to address the more fundamental problems associated with the use of large, coal-fired boilers – availability, and what might be termed 'turn round time'. To raise steam from cold water in a large express locomotive takes from three to five hours; to clean the fire and replenish the coal and water supplies at the end of a run takes forty-five minutes to an hour. With the electric or diesel locomotive these problems are greatly reduced, if not entirely eliminated. O.V.S. Bulleid did begin to address this issue with his 'Leader' class locomotives, and H.G. Ivatt was also cognizant of the difficulties, but both the 'Leader' and the work of Ivatt were little more than a desperate attempt to forestall the inevitability of the demise of the steam locomotive as the major form of traction on the railway network.

Unquestionably there were new developments in almost every area of the railway, new signalling, new types of service, and even new ventures – the Great Western took to the skies and had its own air fleet, though not, of course, a steam-powered one. Ultimately, steam locomotive technology and railway development were both on the wane. The introduction of the electric locomotive and electric colour light signalling, could be cited as new technologies which enhanced railway competitiveness, effectiveness and safety, but it is still the same railway system, with the same inherent limitations. Goods still have to be unloaded from wagons into railway trucks and from them back into wagons, though containerization has gone some way to reducing this particular difficulty. The other well-known form of railway baggage, the traveller, still has to travel to and from the station, not simply get into the car and drive off, and no railway could hope to compete at that level of personal convenience.

The issue of containerization was discussed before an invited audience at the Royal Automobile Club in 1912, with a vast and imaginative scheme being proposed for a new type of goods 'Clearing House'. Containerization was to be a part of the scheme, though it was more than forty years later, with the advent of the liner trains which commenced operations in 1966, before a working container-load system began to operate effectively. There was in this address the 'Life of a Wagon', which, long before Dr Beeching, pointed out that the average goods wagon spent most of its twenty-year life span sat unused in a siding.

The new technologies of the automobile, telephone and electricity were the new areas of investment for the twentieth century; these industries were now the new frontiers which had once been the railways' exclusive territory. The railways did not fail to compete, they failed to see where their strengths were and exhausted themselves in trying to win a market in which they could not compete, not because they lacked the resources but because they could never match the level of personal convenience afforded by the motor car. Similar difficulties existed in relation to a large proportion of the railways' freight business, in some areas even the bicycle could be seen as a threat to the railways' commuter traffic. It also needs to be said that the railways also continued to spend money attempting to develop steam technology instead of investing in the development of the new forms of traction of diesel and especially electric locomotives, specifically adapted and suited to railway use.

The decline, the first glimmers of which were visible by the time of the 1895 races, was slow at first, a growing population and increased levels of manufacture helped to mask the problems, as did the new and more efficient locomotives, carrying greater payloads at higher average speeds. Many regard the period between the 1895 races and the outbreak of the Second World War as the heyday of railway travel both in terms of locomotive development and railway supremacy. However, the railways' financial position and their status as measured by the size and worth of the companies themselves tell a different story.

> It is sometimes forgotten, amid the sad retraction from the kaleidoscope of the pre-grouping railways, that grouping was done to try and make the railways pay.
>
> Bulleid, *Master Builders of Steam*, p. 55

It also has to be said that never again did any company match the record of the West Coast companies, in terms of reliability and speed over such distances and durations as were achieved during the weeks between 14 July and 23 August 1895, though services like the 'Mid-Day Scot' from Euston to Glasgow and the 'Flying Scotsman' between King's Cross and Edinburgh Waverley were very close contenders.

The high speeds set during the races of 1895 were maintained in some measure only in 1900 by the Caledonian who were running a mile-a-minute timing over a 30 mile stretch. In 1905 the North Eastern joined the Caledonian as it increased the speeds of some services and began running a scheduled service which, from Darlington to York, averaged 61.5 m.p.h. Over the next thirty years this average rose to 70.4 m.p.h. for not only the Darlington–York section, but for the whole 232.3 miles between King's Cross and Darlington. The comparison between the increased average speeds during the race and the rise achieved in the ensuing forty years is very noticeable. In 1895, in the space of six weeks, average speeds rose from a low of just under 50 m.p.h. to long-distance averages around 65 m.p.h., and point-to-point averages as high as 82 m.p.h. Increases in average speeds, like those achieved in the races, reflect how slow the progress of raising the average speeds became after the racing ended.

At the outbreak of hostilities in 1939 the fastest scheduled speed was the 71.9 m.p.h. average between King's Cross and York. This level of speed was the exception rather than the rule and it was kept by just one service, the 4 p.m. ex-King's Cross, though there were two runs with averages of 70.4 m.p.h. on the East Coast route and there was one of 71.4 m.p.h. being made between Swindon and Paddington on the Great Western. There were a further thirty-two runs scheduled at speeds of more than a mile a minute over the East Coast route between King's Cross and Edinburgh or points in between. On the West Coast the figures were broadly similar, forty runs over the race route or part of it at a mile a minute or more, though the highest average speeds were not quite up to the East Coast figures – the best West Coast figure being only 65.1 m.p.h. whereas the East Coast had six runs at average speeds of more than 66 m.p.h. The 71.9 m.p.h. of the London & North Eastern using steam does not compare too favourably with the averages set by the 'Zephyr' in America, which was running at an almost 78 m.p.h. average speed between Denver and Chicago in 1934, nor those of the 'Flying Hamburger' service in Germany, both of which were using diesel traction.

The Second World War wrecked any possibility of improving on the 1939 schedules and as late as 1967, even with diesel traction, these pre-war levels had hardly altered. The highest average then being maintained was 73.7 m.p.h., again over the King's Cross–Darlington route, but this was only 3.3 m.p.h. faster than in 1935 and a mere 10 m.p.h. greater than the West Coast race record of 63.7 m.p.h. for the 540 mile journey, undertaken seventy-two years earlier.

The 1960s brought further changes with new types of electric traction coming into use over the former London & North Western metals between Euston, Manchester and Liverpool. The new 25 kV alternating current electric locomotives pushed the average speed, over the 163.2 miles between Watford and Runcorn, to 81.9 m.p.h. Fast as this seems, it can be measured against a run at an average speed of 81.6 m.p.h. between Swindon and Paddington made in 1932, though of course, this was a one-off event and those of the electric locomotive were the scheduled times.

Before dealing with the changes brought about through the increased use of electrification, there have been a number of other contests involving pitting one locomotive against another which need to be mentioned, though these events were not conducted in the same manner as that which prevailed in the races. These latter-day contests took several different forms, some based on comparative exchanges, others on flat-out speeds over short distances and perhaps the most 'romantic' of all, the high-speed, non-stop running of the streamlining era in the 1930s. The London & North Western could be described as a pioneer of the long-distance non-stop run:

Having made the fastest run ever recorded over such a distance as 299 miles, on the night of August 22nd, when the Aberdeen 'flyer' reached Carlisle at 12.35a.m., at an average speed of 65.3m.p.h., they then proceeeed [*sic*] to show that the North Western, alone among the railways of the world, could run the same distance non-stop! This run was made with a special train, weighing 151 tons, leaving Euston at 8.45a.m. The engine selected was a three-cylinder compound, No. 1305 *Ionic*, and C.J. Alcock, who saw the train leave Euston, has told me how astonished he was to see special wire supports erected on the tender so that coal could be stacked much higher than usual. The *Ionic* was manned by the famous crew of *Hardwicke*'s final racing run, Driver

B. Robinson, and Fireman Wolstenholme [presumably Wolstencroft?]. The non-stop run was successfully made at an average speed of 51m.p.h., bringing the train into Carlisle at 2.38p.m.

Nock, *Railway Race to the North*, p. 126

The fact that this run was undertaken by the pairing of Robinson and Wolstencroft does lend weight to the idea that despite the link system of work allocation, specially chosen crews were used when managers felt the occasion demanded. This was almost certainly the case in 1938 when *Mallard* made her record and big-end-breaking run to achieve the world record for steam locomotive haulage of 126 m.p.h. on the descent from Stoke summit to Essendine.

The London & North Western may have pioneered the long-distance non-stop service at the end of the nineteenth century though, of course, the Americans would perhaps claim that this was their invention. They were running the Chicago Limited with two 130 mile sections and one of 146 miles, and in 1876 had managed to run a very special charter train 439.5 miles non-stop. Whatever the competing claims for the introduction of long-distance non-stop running, the London & North Eastern Railway must take first prize in the twentieth century for the most novel solution to the need to change crews on long, non-stop journeys – the corridor tender. The tenders of several batches of London & North Eastern Pacifics were fitted with a vestibule corridor which allowed a relief crew to travel for part of the journey in the train and then move onto the footplate during the running. It is possible to make an interesting comparison between the running of the 'Flying Scotsman' (as the 10 a.m. ex-King's Cross was known), which ran, in the summer timetable, non-stop from King's Cross to Edinburgh Waverley, and the race train of 1895. The average speed of 63.7 m.p.h., set by the West Coast in the early hours of the morning of 23 August, for the 540 miles between Euston and Aberdeen is almost precisely matched by the average set on a run by the British Railways 'Flying Scotsman' service being logged by Nock almost sixty years later:

In the later years the schedule of the summer non-stop was gradually reduced till in 1954 it was no more than 6½ hours involving an average speed of 60.4mph. It remained the world's record non-stop run with steam, and that fast overall time did not represent the maximum of which the A4 engines were capable. On-time arrivals after delays of 10 to 15 minutes en route were frequent. I have not been able to ascertain the fastest end-to-end time ever made, but a journey of my own provided a net gain of no less than 21 minutes on schedule; 369min for the 392.7 miles, and an average speed of 63.8mph.

Nock, *Speed Records on Britain's Railways*, p. 191

Despite the changes in locomotive design, track improvements, two changes of ownership (the latter into public hands), new signalling, and innumerable changes of management personnel, the average speed of the world's most famous train was scheduled at no quicker speeds than those of sixty years earlier – further evidence, if any were needed, of the contention that the events of 1895 represent a zenith in steam railway operating in Britain.

The streamlining era of the 1930s was used by both East and West Coast routes as a selling point and the use of streamlining was not restricted to the railways of Britain, as locomotive engineers worldwide experimented with new ways to improve the efficiency of their machines. In Britain the end results of the streamlining experiment were relatively inconclusive, though there were savings in horsepower shown in model tests at the National Physical Laboratory's wind-tunnel. However, with full-scale locomotives in service conditions and with all other cost factors brought in, the savings in horsepower were not translated into financial economy. Perhaps the sales angle drew in more passengers and thus increased revenue, though the reductions in cost saved through fuel efficiency or lowered drag and rolling resistance factors, were not creating sufficient savings to appreciably alter the steadily declining ratio between operating costs and income revenues.

The whole saga of *Mallard*'s World Speed Record is an example of how the railways in Britain, or at least the LNER, dealt with the advent of new technologies. Sir Nigel Gresley, chief mechanical engineer to the London & North Eastern, and the man to whom he was responsible, chief general manager Sir Ralph Wedgwood, were more concerned to beat the German record for steam traction than in developing a diesel service to compete against the 'Flying Hamburger' diesel multiple unit service. Thus they pumped more time and money into a form of motive power far less efficient than that beginning to be employed in ever-increasing numbers on lines throughout Europe and North America.

In certain respects this incident can be considered as a classic example of short-sightedness. As has already been mentioned, the French set up a testing plant at Vitry-sur-Seine and the chief mechanical engineers of Britain's railways wanted to construct one in England. A site was agreed at Crossgates on the outskirts of Leeds, Nigel Gresley and Henry Fowler drew up the plans, and costs were estimated at £90,000. This was in June 1930.

> But there were signs of a slump, and of course it was hopelessly out of character to push ahead with anything important when time is on your side and labour is otherwise unemployed.
>
> Bulleid, *Master Builders of Steam*, p. 62

The irony of Bulleid's remarks over the setting up of a testing plant are underlined if the *Mallard* incident is examined further.

> Whilst the 'Cock o' the North' design was taking shape in Doncaster drawing office, and later whilst the engine was showing its paces, Gresley was weighing up two advances indicated by this design – increased power and the undoubted practicability of progressing from a smooth external casing to more complete streamlining which would save power at high speeds. He

*1988 was more than the centenary of the race to Edinburgh, it was also the fiftieth anniversary of* Mallard's *126 m.p.h. record-breaking run and the 150th anniversary of the Mail Train. No. 4468* Mallard *is hauling a special commemorative train between Manchester and York, which was part of a whole series of events linked to the post office and* Mallard's *record. The scene is just a few yards from what was once the original terminus of the Selby & Leeds Railway at Marsh Lane in Leeds. The object above and to the rear of the lamp is a pennant in the form of a postage stamp. The shiny quartering on the buffers is the sort of thing driver Soutar was paying the engine cleaners to do, back in 1895.*

accordingly pointed out to his Chief General Manager, Sir Ralph Wedgwood, that there was scope for an extra-high-speed train on the King's Cross–Newcastle run – averaging, say, 70 mph so as to cover the 268 miles in four hours with a stop at Darlington. He visualised the project as a complete train, and he visited Germany to obtain first hand experience of a similar project, the Flying Hamburger. In October 1934 this was a well-established high-speed diesel train, booked to average 74mph on the comparatively easy road between Berlin and Hamburg: Gresley was most impressed by the smooth running at 100mph and he placed a firm enquiry for the supply of a complete train for the Newcastle run. Detailed proposals for a 115 ton diesel-engined train of three articulated coaches with 140 seats came back, with calculations suggesting a booked time of 4 hrs. 15min. for the journey. 'Interesting,' said Wedgwood, 'but you could operate a more comfortable train with more seats to a faster schedule with one of your ordinary Pacifics.

Bulleid, *Master Builders of Steam*, p. 65

*Sir Ralph Wedgwood, chief general manager of the London & North Eastern Railway during the streamlining era and Gresley's attempts on the World Speed Record for steam locomotion. (National Railway Museum)*

Wedgwood's reported comments fail entirely to take account of the differences in availability, or savings in track maintenance from reduced 'hammer blow', nor those resulting from the reduction in footplate crew, shed staff and other grades, made possible by the use of diesel power. Wedgwood's remarks, and Gresley's subsequent actions, point towards a failure by both men to get to grips with the emerging technological advances. Thus they continued to develop the steam-powered railway, despite the savings in labour and material costs offered by expanding the use of either diesel or electric power; this was in use on the Southern Railway's Brighton main line in 1934, therefore both men must have been aware of at least some of the possibilities of these forms of traction. If the Grouping was an attempt to make the railways pay, the continued research and development of steam power was hardly the way forward.

In the teeth of those who will not hear a word against Sir Nigel Gresley I assert that few men have done greater disservice to British Railways than when he proved to the Board of the L.N.E.R. that they should continue with their policy of steam traction. . . .

Gresley condemned us to around 2,000 h.p. when we needed over 3,000 for twenty unnecessary years.

Fiennes, *I Tried to Run a Railway*, p. 66

Fiennes's criticism of Gresley, justified though it may be, should not be limited to Gresley nor simply to locomotive policy, for there were other aspects of management equally at fault, not only in relation to being persuaded to stick with steam, but also by way of organizational errors:

> When the L.N.E.R. was formed in 1923 Sir Ralph Wedgewood set up at King's Cross his own Chief General Manager's office, consisting of his personal staff, a staff section, a works office, an industrial agent and little else: not more than about 40 all told. He delegated the general and functional management of the railway to three Divisional General Managers, Southern, North Eastern and Scottish. Each of these three officers directed and controlled the activities of a commercial, an operating and a loco running superintendent. Sir Ralph did not therefore present in his organisation one of the first principals of good timetables, that both terminals of a service should be under the same manager. Newcastle was separated from King's Cross, Leeds from Edinburgh. Later still [after nationalization] Sir Brian Robertson was responsible for worse, separating Leeds from King's Cross.

> Fiennes, *I Tried to Run a Railway*, pp. 64–5

Arguments over the type of motive power notwithstanding the streamlined train did enter service, and the methods used in promoting the service to the public were once again those of the speed of the service, with the reduction of journey time and/or overall average speed being quoted in posters promoting the services. The poster advertising the 'Coronation Scot' proclaimed: 'Streamlined Restaurant Car Express, London & Glasgow in 6½ Hours, average speed throughout 61.7 m.p.h.' The year was 1939, and the overall average was 2 m.p.h. slower than that of the race in 1895! The inauguration of these high-speed, luxury, streamlined services was usually preceded by the running of a test-train and even a special press train to ensure maximum coverage – an event which is still used in 1990s Britain.

The contest surrounding the streamlined services was again very much an East Coast versus West Coast contest, though the Great Western did make a token gesture by adding a bullet front and various fins and fairings to 'Castle' class engine No. 5005 *Manorbier Castle* and to the 'King' class engine No. 6014 *King Henry VII*. These additions did not enhance their appearance and the Great Western did not pursue the matter further.

The streamlining era was influenced not only by engineering principals or savings of horsepower but, like the designers before them, Gresley, Bulleid and Stanier had an aesthetic as well as purely utilitarian view of the locomotives they designed, and in the designs of the streamlining era the origins of that aestheticism lie within the ambit of the art deco movement. Nowhere is this more apparent than in the 'Merchant Navy', 'Battle of Britain' and 'West Country' class locomotives of O.V.S. Bulleid, Gresley's former assistant, who was made chief mechanical engineer of the Southern Railway in 1938. The first of Bulleid's 'Merchant Navy' class, No. 21C1 *Channel Packet*, entered service three years later in 1941.

*The Southern Region of British Railways sent one of its Bulleid Pacifics to the Scottish Region in 1948. The crew of this particular engine, No. 34004 Yeovil, were a pair of Nine Elms men, driver Swain and fireman Bert Hooker, who is now a railway author himself. This crew knew their locomotive would not be the most economical and so they chose to show the Scottish crews what their engine was capable of and created some spirited running in the process. This engine, No. 34092 City of Wells, is fitted with the Giesel ejector in place of the original Le Maitre multi-jet blastpipe. The art deco influence can be seen in the shaping of the streamlining; it is officially known as 'air smoothed' casing.*

Gresley's design for his streamlined 'A4' class Pacifics was influenced by the Bugatti-designed railcars for French railways. However, the overall design of locomotive and train was very much in keeping not only with art deco styles, but colour schemes too. One thing which can be said in favour of British locomotive designers is that they did give more consideration to the aesthetic appearance of their locomotives than was the case in many other railway systems throughout the world.

This period from the lessening of the Depression to the outbreak of the Second World War did witness some exciting events in relation to ever-higher maximum speeds. In the years between the end of the races of 1895 and the First World War there are several claims to have reached and surpassed 100 m.p.h., including *City of Truro* and a locomotive on the Penn State railroad in America. There was little change in this figure until the years 1935 to 1938 when the Gresley Class 'A3' and 'A4' Pacifics Nos 2750 *Papyrus*, 2509 *Silver Link*, 2512 *Silver Fox* and then, finally, No. 4468 *Mallard* took the records to respectively 108 m.p.h., 112.5 m.p.h., 113 m.p.h. and the all-time record of 126 m.p.h. Sandwiched in between these are the efforts of Sir William Arthur Stanier's Pacific No. 6220 *Coronation*, which held the British top speed record for a period during 1937 and early 1938 of 114 m.p.h.

Fine though the efforts were to create a high-speed steam-hauled service on Britain's railways, they represent little more than an Indian summer. At the end of

*Stanier's Pacific, another of the locomotive types which were trialists in the 1948 exchanges, is captured here on a Friends of the National Railway Museum Rail Tour organized to celebrate her return to steam after a major overhaul, for which the friends had raised much of the £250,000 spent in putting the locomotive back into full main line working condition.*

the Second World War the railways were in a parlous state, as were numerous other areas of social life and housing. The difficulties of returning troops and persuading women back into the home after their war work in all manner of industries from farming to railway work were part of the difficulties, and shortages of all kinds were another. In what may only be described as the most difficult of circumstances, in 1947 the newly elected Labour government chose to put the railways into public ownership and on 1 January 1948, along with the mines, the railways were nationalized, being put under the control of the British Transport Commission.

The racing fever of earlier decades was still not dead and it too re-emerged, disguised as the 'Locomotive Exchanges', which were ostensibly designed to help the newly formed BTC select 'Standard' designs for British Railways. However, these trials provided yet another excuse to pit one engine against another in competition, not vastly different from those held to determine which designer would provide the motive power for the Liverpool & Manchester back in 1829. These trials resulted in the British Railway Standard types designed under the leadership of R.A. Riddles, who had previously had responsibility for locomotive design during the period of the Second World War, when the railways were under government control.

The newly nationalized railway system attempted to re-create something of the pre-war flavour with the reinstatement of the non-stop London–Edinburgh service in May 1948, though speeds were not those of the pre-war period. Every effort was made to speed up and improve services in the 1950s, but the attempts were hindered by changes of government, changes of policy and a lack of capital resources to upgrade the system or improve the motive power situation. The decision to electrify the West Coast route was taken in principal in 1956, though it was not until ten years later that the services became fully electrified between London and Manchester and Liverpool, and longer still was taken to electrify the route right through to Glasgow, which was only completed in 1975. Continuing to uphold the old traditions, high-speed runs were made over the newly electrified route and, though the East Coast route did not have electrification in 1966, they had introduced the 'Deltic' class diesels on the King's Cross–Edinburgh and King's Cross–Leeds services in 1962, and had made high-speed special runs to exploit media coverage.

The whole history of railway affairs has been littered with every conceivable form of management error, from the failings associated with a top down autocratic style, to collective failures of nerve when faced with crucial decisions on policy issues such as duplication of routes and motive-power design. Only government interference in railway affairs has a more salubrious record than their military-style management and following the changes of 1948 the railways became even more of a political football. Ideologically, from the perspective of at least one political party and countless highly paid and influential industrialists, nationalization could not be seen to succeed and political and ideological requirements came to take on more weight than the judgements of highly trained and lifelong railwaymen.

It is one of the disasters about British Railways that in the years between 1947 and 1955 no one had done the basic work on what we were there for at

*'Out to grass', Britain's last steam locomotive No. 92220* Evening Star. *Completed in 1962 this huge locomotive had a working life of less than seven years, though realistically it should have had one of at least thirty to forty. That it did not is cause for concern.*

all; what traffic should be carried by what methods in what quantities, where from and to, at what rates. The upshot was that the Modernisation Plan produced in 1953–55 with the support of the Government to the extent of 1,500m. was little more than a change from steam traction plus a host of mouldering schemes which the B.T.C. and the Regions had found after a hurried search in their pigeon holes. We had made the basic error of buying our tools before doing our homework on defining the job.

Fiennes, I Tried to Run a Railway, pp. 76–7

Failure to do basic business and market research was not new to the railways – it had been one of their failings for years and now it was not the only way in which the railways' problems intensified. An example of the difficulty the network faced can be seen in the dispute between Dr Beeching and Lord Robens over the introduction of the 'Merry-go-Round', trains taking coal direct from the pit to the power station virtually without a stop.

The great and good Doctor was rightly critical of our enormous fleet of wagons. Some types made no more than 20 journeys per year. At no type and at no aspect of that type's operation did he gnash his teeth more frequently and more loudly than at the mineral wagon and its habit of spending most of the summer doing nothing at all and for a not inconsiderable part of the winter in sidings at collieries waiting to be loaded and labelled. The capital sum involved in these wagons was around 400m.

'You shall pay for this,' said Dr. B. to Lord Robens. 'Ten million pounds a year and cheap at the price.'

'What?' said Lord Robens, 'And pay as well to re-equip most of my long-life collieries with bunkers for your blasted merry-go-round. No, Sir!'

In vain I argued that their argument was unreal. It was a paper transfer from the pocket of one nationalised industry to another; whereas my case was not only one of a direct and solid contribution to the productivity of both industries, let alone the nation; but would make their other argument unnecessary. Merry-go-Round in itself would reduce the fleet of mineral wagons from around half a million to around 100,000. It was no use. Five Years.

Fiennes, I Tried to Run a Railway, p. 81

Conveniently, this dispute was damaging to not one but two nationalized industries, and both Beeching and Robens were political appointments made by a government ideologically antipathetic to the success of nationalization. The increased political interference in railway affairs since 1948 has had disastrous consequences, not only for the railway but also for the taxpayer, who has been obliged to foot the bill for both errors of management and political dogma. However, despite all the vicissitudes of this unfortunate situation, the spirit of high-speed running did not disappear and, even at this very late stage in the steam-driven age, there were some splendid efforts made by individual enginemen and, railway man that he was, Fiennes could not resist telling of one such deed.

The driver in Fiennes's tale was a man by the name of W. (Bill) Hoole, and the running in question was not with an express passenger train but an express freight. The route was the East Coast main line between London and Retford. Driver Hoole had a train of some forty-seven wagons weighing around 450 tons and his engine was one of Gresley's Pacifics. First, driver Hoole outran the 3.40 p.m. King's Cross–Leeds, but then had to stop at Peterborough to detach a wagon with a hot box.

The signal remained at danger, not only while the 3.40 went by but also the Talisman. Then the board came off and Bill opened the regulator. The Talisman averages nearly 80 mile an hour beyond Peterborough. It took Bill nearly to Retford to run him down. I began to have doubts about safety.

Fiennes, I Tried to Run a Railway, p. 71

Driver Hoole's efforts cannot be regarded as merely an isolated incident; there were many other crews who did their utmost to run the services to time, making up delays wherever possible. I can speak from direct personal experience of workings over the Waterloo–Bournemouth and Waterloo–Salisbury routes, during the last years of steam services over these lines. Indeed, things went beyond making up lost time, and there were certain services on which some crews quite actively competed against each other for the fastest possible time between Waterloo and Basingstoke. This was all being done in the full knowledge that the steam locomotive was going for good, and this would be the last possible chance to see what Bulleid's Pacifics could do.

It is tempting to say that as long as there are railways there will be footplatemen prepared to run hard and fast, though with driverless trains a commonplace, how long there will be footplatemen is itself a moot point. The advent of diesel and electric traction removed the need for a fireman on the footplate (or, rather, in the cab). It may only be a matter of time before the railway equivalent of *Star Trek*'s Mr Data makes the driver redundant too.

The 'modernization' of British Railways suffered many of the iniquities of progress by committee, political interference in operational issues, and underfunding on a massive scale.

> From its inception, the financial structure of British Rail carried a number of serious handicaps. First, the relationship between the capitalisation of the business and its earning power, if any did exist, was accidental. The British Transport Commission took over from the four main-line railways a rag-bag of assets, worn out by the war, and in the main unprofitable in the last years of normal operation before the war. The Commission's capital structure, on which interest was to be paid to the Treasury, was based on the share prices of the former main line railway companies.
>
> With hindsight, it is obvious that a set of assets which after heavy investment could produce results like those of the late Fifties and Sixties was, in aggregate, worth no more than scrap value at January 1st, 1948. But these assets were taken into the accounts at their values in the accounts of the former main line companies, i.e. 941 million, financed, in the main, by three per cent Transport Stock. In addition, the Commission's operations were expected to provide for the amortisation of the capital debt over 99 years.
>
> Joy, *The Train that Ran Away*, p. 13

Dr Joy continues his demolition of the financial failings of British Rail by reference to past performances and to the underlying causes of the railway's problems:

> The railway industry in Britain had been in economic difficulty since World War I. Even before the spread of motor vehicles, there had been, in aggregate, too much railway capacity, but the competitive structure of the industry prevented anything being done about it.
>
> Joy, *The Train that Ran Away*, p. 13

The very way in which the British railway network came into being was, in essence, the very reason for its poor performance throughout the twentieth century. The duplication of routes, the building of routes for the sole reason of thwarting competitors, and the opening of lines based upon nothing more than speculation, was the direct consequence of the policy of *laissez-faire* practised in relation to railway company expansion throughout the Victorian period. Though not all of the most speculative lines were built, this did not stop them being a cause of loss for those who had invested in them. The really important decisions about the railway have been constantly fudged. The fudging is a variation on the death-by-a-thousand-cuts scenario and, over the years, it has been the cause of the haemorrhaging of huge amounts of capital, both public and private, and the process shows little sign of altering or abating; waste and missed opportunity on this scale is little short of insanity.

> The main problem was that Britain's railways, like those of the USA, were over built. This was the price of competitive development of the systems. Most other countries had seen the error of 19th century Britain's policy and had exercised strict control over the construction of railways.
>
> Joy, *The Train that Ran Away*, p. 23

The races of 1888 and, more especially, those of 1895 were the most public manifestations of the high degree of competitiveness that infected British railways; a competitiveness that was historic in origin and ruinous in nature. In previous chapters the question of who won was raised and, indeed, credence was given to the West Coast route's claims in this matter. However, there were no real winners; no financial benefits were derived from the racing and, eventually, both routes and all the companies involved were merged into greater wholes. These new, regional monopolies failed to address the issues posed by new technology – the changing nature of the real competition, the question of duplication of routes, and the overmanning which resulted from the failure of management to see the threats to, and weaknesses of, their business. The four regional monopolies became the four regional divisions under nationalization, though this changed nothing as has already been stated.

The railway industry, which in many respects began its very existence in Britain, is a microcosm of British business and political life from the beginnings of the nineteenth century to the present time. The growth, consolidation, maturity and decline of the British railway industry and the national railway system mirrors the growth, maturity and decline of Empire, of manufacturing capacity and economic standing. The mistakes made, though in many ways avoided by Britain's international competitors, still continue to be made here, and the débâcle over the high-speed rail link to the Channel is yet another classic example, matched only by the failure to address the real problem of the railways. Instead of putting in place a genuine, national transport policy, as the British Transport Commission should have done in the 1950s, now the way forward is a pathetic attempt to sell off those parts of the system which can be made viably economic. The initial nineteenth-century mistake of allowing utterly unfettered railway speculation has continually been compounded by political expediency, and by financial incompetence, at times on a breathtaking scale – some £2.5 billion between 1956 and 1968, if Dr Joy's figures are to be taken as correct.

Leaving aside the vicissitudes of policy and incompetence, the ripples of 1895 are still visible as the age of the electric railway enters its second decade in Britain. Following the electrification of the West Coast Route and the widespread dieselization of the rest of the national network, 'new' developments in high-speed running were being investigated. The French who, as early as 1955, had set a remarkable record of 331 k.p.h. with electric traction, and the Japanese who in 1964 were running a 210 k.p.h. service train, were showing the way forward for railway travel. The very high speed, set by the French in 1955, was very close to the limits: the track, catenary and pantograph were all damaged but, rather than abandoning the idea, new ways were sought to overcome the difficulties.

In Japan the 'Shinkansen', as the 210 k.p.h. service was known, was so heavy on the track that it was closed each night for maintenance. Despite these obstacles, work on raising speeds continued and, in 1967, British Rail began development of the Advanced Passenger Train. Though the initial designs for the APT proved less than successful they did form the basis for the introduction of the High Speed Train, which began its career in 1976 on the Paddington–West of England routes. In 'trials' the prototype HST was run at 143 m.p.h. and they have become popularly known as the '125' trains. The sagas of the APT and the HST are further examples of the failings of management, railway engineers and the government.

The French, with their Train Grand Vitesse or TGV, were up and running in 1972, taking their test train to 318 k.p.h. or almost 200 m.p.h. In service, the TGV operates at a maximum of 270 k.p.h. Some idea of the savings in journey time created by the TGV can be gained from the fact that the Paris–Geneva journey time fell from 6 hours 25 minutes to 3 hours 30 minutes. The introduction of the TGV services created a 14 per cent increase in passenger numbers; this compares with an increase of 20 per cent seen on the introduction of the 'Deltic' hauled services on the East Coast main line. It would seem that however high speeds may go there will be passengers wishing to travel – which brings us full circle, right back to the remarks of the epitome of Victorian railwaymen, Isambard Kingdom Brunel:

> The public will always prefer that conveyance which is the most perfect; and speed, within reasonable limits, is a material ingredient in perfection of travelling.

> Nock, *The Railway Engineers*, 1955), p. 251

The publicity value of the high-speed service is as important today as it was in 1895. It could be argued that the fascination with speed is endemic, after all there have been incidences and reports of high-speed running since the railways began, and even the 270 k.p.h. speeds of the TGV look positively slow against the 500 k.p.h. services which could be introduced if the 'Maglev' project, being developed in Japan, comes to fruition. The question is whether the 'Maglev' qualifies as a

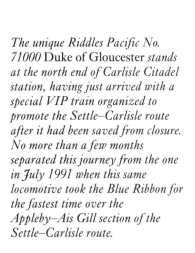

*The unique Riddles Pacific No. 71000* Duke of Gloucester *stands at the north end of Carlisle Citadel station, having just arrived with a special VIP train organized to promote the Settle–Carlisle route after it had been saved from closure. No more than a few months separated this journey from the one in July 1991 when this same locomotive took the Blue Ribbon for the fastest time over the Appleby–Ais Gill section of the Settle–Carlisle route.*

railway, for only at the beginning and end of its journey, when it is speeding up or slowing down, does it actually touch a track of any sort and when running at service speed it is literally floating on a magnetic field – hence 'Maglev'.

The latest developments in electric traction travel at speeds unimaginable in Brunel's day, but locomotives that Brunel would be quite at home with are still operational and the spirit of record making and high-speed running is still to be found among the current British Rail footplatemen.

Since the ending of steam as the tractive force on British Rail in 1968, the use of steam locomotives has been confined to special services run as tourist attractions or for the benefit of steam locomotive enthusiasts. One of the steam-hauled services, run on a regular basis as both tourist attraction and enthusiast special, is the 'Cumbrian Mountain Express' which is steam hauled over the famous Settle–Carlisle route of the former Midland Railway. On this service there is in existence an 'unofficial' Blue Ribbon competition for the best climb from the standing start at Appleby to the line's summit at Ais Gill in the high Pennines.

Though the steam services are limited to 70 m.p.h., the ascent to Ais Gill does not test all-out speed but pulling power, adhesion and the boiler's capacity to produce steam. The contest for the Appleby–Ais Gill climb is waged between the locomotives of all of the major locomotive designers from the last days of the Grouping and the first days of British Rail: Gresley, Stanier, Bulleid, Riddles and Peppercorn. The engines involved in the contest have been restored and are kept

*This is one 'made earlier'; built in the year of nationalization this was the first locomotive to emerge from the workshops at Doncaster carrying a 'British Railways' number. Named* Blue Peter, *No. 60532 was saved from the cutter's torch by the Blue Peter Locomotive Society and is seen here at Shipley Bingley Junction, bound for Carlisle. Had the London & North Eastern Railway not continued with the futile development of the steam locomotive it is unlikely that No. 60532 and the other engines of her class would ever have been built.*

in operating condition by the enthusiasts who have even gone so far as to carry out improvements to the original designs.

R.A. Riddles, whose desire to be the last great steam locomotive engineer was yet another reason for the delay in adopting modern forms of traction, was responsible for the introduction into service of the unique engine No. 71000 *Duke of Gloucester*. This engine was to be the prototype for a new fleet of steam-powered express engines incorporating all the latest steam technology; in reality it was nothing of the sort, and in its original form was little better than a white elephant. However, thanks to the dedicated work of numerous enthusiasts, this engine was not only saved from extinction, but was modified and improved by its rescuers to the point where it became a contender for the Appleby–Ais Gill Blue Ribbon and, in July 1991, succeeded in snatching the ribbon from the Stanier Pacific No. 46229 *Duchess of Hamilton*. From a standing start at Appleby No. 71000 *Duke of Gloucester* cleared the summit at 60 m.p.h., with an average speed between mileposts 259¾ and 275 of 55 m.p.h. The driver on both the *Duchess of Hamilton*'s run and that of the *Duke of Gloucester* was Willie Alexander, and his fireman was Paul Kane.

The efforts of No. 71000 *Duke of Gloucester* and No. 46229 *Duchess of Hamilton* have been matched by those of Peppercorn's Pacific No. 60532 *Blue Peter* and, at various times, all three engines have held the record for the Ais Gill ascent. Though it is impossible to compare the limited journeys made by these engines with those of a 540 mile race held one hundred years ago in 1895, the spirit of the footplate crews remains. Running of the type made by the three Pacifics is, in many ways, the direct descendant of the efforts made during the races of 1895 and, it has to be said, it has little to do with management, government or increased traffic, and everything to do with pride, achievement and not a little romance.

# APPENDIX

## SIMILARITIES AND CONNECTIONS BETWEEN 1895 AND 1995

Anyone considering that progress has been made and that things are no longer carried out in the same way as they were in 1895 and earlier, should ponder the way in which the Channel Tunnel and the high-speed links between it and the rest of Britain are being developed. The speed of trains is not the only issue still resembling the 1890s – safety matters are now treated by the government in the same way as they once were by the former railway companies. The Hidden report, produced as a result of the enquiry into the 1988 Clapham rail crash, has not only not yet been acted upon, it is unlikely now that it will be.

> A 700 million hi-tech safety scheme designed to reduce railway accidents has been scrapped by the Government. The decision has been taken on 'value for money grounds' . . . Ministers have decided they cannot justify the high cost of installing the scheme, recommended by the Hidden report . . .
>
> *The Guardian*, 28 February 1995, p. 7

The implementation of the Hidden report is not only about improvements in signalling and computer-controlled train safety devices, it also covers areas such as the chronic overcrowding on the commuter services into London. Capital Transport Campaign, a commuter pressure group, claims that overcrowding, which leads to large numbers of standing passengers, is currently three times the safety limits recommended in the Hidden report. The parallels between the attitudes of the railway companies in the Victorian era and those currently responsible for the running and administration of the railway network are so numerous as to be, perhaps, the one area in which it can be said that there has been a return to Victorian values.

Railtrack, the body responsible for the track and signalling, is now being asked to work with the Railway Inspectorate to produce a list of black spots where the new system can be installed, at a cost of £8 million, very reminiscent of the saga of chain brakes and non-automatic vacuum brakes, only now with twentieth-century technology instead of nineteenth.

Why £700 million cannot be justified on passenger safety, yet £1.4 billion can be justified in debt write-offs to make the railway a more attractive privatization cherry, on top of £200 million spent on consultants to tell the government how to privatize the railway, is a question to ponder, perhaps as you head for the Channel Tunnel.

The government has spent eight years deciding which route to endorse and, even in February 1995, the decision was still not absolutely final. Despite being on land, the high-speed link from the Channel Tunnel to London will entail as much tunnelling as the Channel Tunnel itself, much of which is to cover objections to the route as to any engineering difficulties. Another of the reasons that route planning has been fraught is that an international station has been constructed in Ashford and for some time one of the preferred routes meant trains would have to divert to call at the new station or miss stopping at the new and expensive Ashford International station altogether.

The privatization dogma has been another major stumbling block for this route, as it has been for investment in the railways in general. At first the government said that the high-speed Channel Tunnel link would have to be financed through private sector enterprise, though they did relent slightly in 1994 and will now make some form of capital available for the project, on which a considerable amount has already been spent. £750,000 has been spent on models of the route, which were used in more than a thousand public meetings held to determine the route and its effects on people's properties and livelihoods. In addition to this huge public relations exercise, there have been over 2½ million boreholes made to ascertain the nature of the terrain that the line and its accompanying tunnels will have to pass through. These holes all have to be paid for, as does the acre of linen that has been used already in preparing parliamentary bills, which are submitted on linen backings just as they were when Railway Mania was in full swing, back in 1846. All this activity and the delays involved has swallowed up huge amounts of money without producing so much as a foot of track, in much the same way as the London & York Bill and its passage through the House from 1844 to 1846; indeed the London & York Bill was passed in two years whereas the high-speed tunnel link has been on the drawing-board for eight.

There have been trips to France for lawyers and for residents whose homes will be close to the new lines so that they could experience for themselves noise levels generated by the TGV, which will be similar to those of any British service on this route. Once the line is opened the estimated time for the London–Paris journey will be two hours and the increased levels of investment will lead not only to lower journey times but also passenger increases, ushering in 'a new age of the train'. However, on one recent journey the Brussels–London service was running at less than one-third capacity.

The below capacity running may not be unconnected with return fares in the £150 or more bracket, shortages of available luggage space in the specially designed trains, and various restrictions covering return journeys, and this is on the early morning service designed to attract the business user. The interest in these matters from the point of *Racing Trains* is that on the commencement of the Channel Tunnel, services parties of journalists took trains, boats and planes to Paris in a race to see which team would get there first. In the event, the train won, but not without some incident as the specially laid-on train failed to start and the reserve train had to be called for, causing not inconsiderable delay. The railway's blushes were not saved by their own prompt actions, but by staff difficulties at French airports, which created sufficient delay to the air travel team to allow the train users to make good their poor start.

Constructing a high-speed line from London to the Continent is only one part of the railway's operations and at the same time as the Channel Tunnel debate has been raging, there have been numerous discussions on the future of the West Coast route to Scotland, a debate which has been around since at least the 1830s when there were a great many discourses on the advisability of having two separate routes to Scotland. The conclusion one is drawn to is, that like racing trains, arguing about the routes and the services upon them is as old as railways themselves and that, given the present *status quo*, there seems to be every possibility that this situation will continue.

The recently retired former chairman of the British Railways Board, Sir Bob Reid, in a stinging rebuke to Prime Minister Major's criticisms of British Rail's performance, said:

> We now have a structure more complicated than necessary. Our view was subordinated to that of one consultant who has never run anything.
>
> Rebecca Smithers, quoting Sir Bob Reid,
> *The Guardian*, 25 February 1995, p. 6

The real issues surrounding the railway are not those of ownership, they are about competent management, planned and properly accounted investment, and the social and environmental priorities of a genuine national transport policy. Cooperation and the coordination of an efficient distributive system are more important issues than ownership. For too long the railway has been a black hole into which vast sums of taxpayers' money has disappeared, though disappeared is perhaps not the right word. Vast sums of public money have been paid to consultancies, merchant banks, spin-doctors, advertising agencies and a whole plethora of shapers and shakers, whose entire output has consistently, maybe even deliberately, missed the point – railways have not been a paying proposition for decades, decades during which billions have been spent on creating an alternative system of distribution. Motorways, major trunk routes and bypasses are frequently built, not to benefit the private car user, but to speed the movement of goods and freight which ought properly to have been railway and not road traffic.

In all this senseless wrangling over the wrong questions, one thing that does seem certain is that racing trains in some shape or form is endemic, but never again will major railway companies indulge in all-out racing over a 540 mile race track for little more than the thrill of it. More's the pity.

# BIBLIOGRAPHY

Town of publication is London unless otherwise stated

Acworth, W.M. *The Railways of England*, 1st edn, John Murray, 1900, 5th edn (reprinted), Ian Allan
Allen, C.J. *The Locomotive Exchanges 1870–1948*, Ian Allan, 1949
—— *The North Eastern Railway*, Ian Allan, 1964
Anon. *The Jubilee of Railway News 1864–1914*, Railway News, 1914
—— 'Race to Aberdeen', *Railway Times*, August 1895
—— 'Race to the North', *Railway Times*, July 1895
—— 'Summary & Comparison of U.S.A. and Empire State Express', *Railway Times*, October 1895
Bulleid, H.A.V. *Master Builders of Steam*, Ian Allan, 1963
Chaloner, W.H. 'F.W. Webb (1836–1906) of the London North Western Railway', *Transport History*,
   1 (1968), no. 2
Coleman, T. *The Railway Navvies*, Harmondsworth, Penguin, 1986
Jeremy, D.J. *et al.* (eds) *Dictionary of Business Biography*, Butterworths, 1986
Ellis, C.H. *The North British Railway*, Ian Allan, 1955
—— *The Engineer*, week ending 8 November 1895
Fiennes, G.F. *I Tried to Run a Railway*, Ian Allan, 1967
Fulford, R. *Glyn's 1753–1953*, Macmillan, 1953
Gregg, P. *A Social and Economic History of Britain 1760–1965*, 5th edn (revised), Harrap, 1965
Joy, S. *The Train that Ran Away*, Ian Allan, 1973
Lambert, R.S. *The Railway King 1800–1871*, Allen & Unwin, 1934
Legg, S. *The Railway Book*, Fourth Estate, 1988
Mountfield, D. *The Railway Barons*, Osprey, 1979
Murphy, B. & Field, A. *ASLEF 1880–1980. A Hundred Years of the Locoman's Trade Union*, Aslef,
   1980
Nock, O.S. *The Caledonian Railway*, Ian Allan, 1962
—— *The Great Northern Railway*, Ian Allan, 1958
—— *The Railway Engineers*, Batsford, 1955
—— *Locomotives of the North Eastern Railway*, Ian Allan, 1974
—— *North Western*, Ian Allan, 1968
—— *The Railway Enthusiast's Encyclopedia*, Hutchinson, 1968
—— *The Railway Race to the North*, 2nd edn, Ian Allan, 1962
—— *Scottish Railways*, Nelson & Sons, 1950
—— *Speed Records on Britain's Railways*, Pan, 1971
Ottley, G. *A Bibliography of British Railway History*, 2nd edn, HMSO, 1983
Pollins, H. 'Railway Contractors & Finance of Railway Development', *Transport History*, 3 (1955),
   no. 1
Reed, M.C. *Railways in the Victorian Economy*, David & Charles, 1969
Rolt, L.T.C. *Red for Danger*, 4th edn (revised), Pan, 1982
Rous-Marten, C. *The Engineer*, August 1895
—— *The Engineer*, September 1895

Schivelbusch, W. *The Railway Journey (The Industrialisation of Time and Space in the 19th Century)*, Leamington Spa, Berg, 1986

'Scot'. 'Our Story', *British Railways Staff Magazine* (Scottish Region), 5 (1954)

Scott, W.J. *Great Northern Speeds or the Fastest Running in the World*, Railway Press Co., 1889

—— *Kinnaber*, Railway Press Co., 1895

Spink, J.E. *F.W. Webb, C.M.E. LNWR 1871–1903*, thesis, Hereford College of Education, 1965

Stretton, C.E. *Safe Railway Working*, 3rd edn, Crosby Lockwood & Sons, 1893

Talbot, E. *The London North Western Recalled*, Poole, Oxford Publishing Co., 1987

Thomas, J. *The North British Railway*, vol. 2, Newton Abbot, David & Charles, 1975

Thompson, F.M.L. *The Rise of Respectable Society: A Social History of Victorian Britain, 1830–1900*, Fontana, 1988

Ransome-Wallis, P.R. *Men of the Footplate*, Ian Allan, 1954

Whitehouse, P. & St John Thomas, D. *The Great Days of the Express Trains*, Newton Abbot, David & Charles, 1990

A basic guide to the operation of the steam locomotive with complete explanations of all working parts, together with descriptions of the duties of the crew can be found in:

Wilson, D. *How Steam Locomotives Work*, Hemel Hempstead, Argus, 1993

# INDEX

Page numbers in italics denote illustrations.